ETC.:

A Review of General Semantics

"I hear that some of the readers like the title ETC. and that a few do not. Personally I feel that the publication of the Society could not have a better title . . . In a non-aristotelian, infinite-valued orientation, we do not assume that what we say *can cover* all the characteristics of a situation, and so we remain conscious of a permanent et cetera *instead of having the dogmatic, period-and-stop attitude."*

ALFRED KORZYBSKI
ETC., Vol. I, No. 1 (1943)

Published four times a year: March, June, September, December.

Editorial Office: San Francisco State College, San Francisco 94132, California.

Business Office: 540 Powell Street, San Francisco 94108.

Subscriptions: $4 a year (U.S. or Canada); no extra postage for foreign subscriptions. For rates in Japan, inquire of the Japan Language Society, 3-23-3 Taka-ban-cho, Meguro-ku, Tokyo. Microfilm edition for subscribing libraries: University Microfilms, 313 N. First St., Ann Arbor, Michigan.

Distribution: Eastern News Company, 311 W. 11th Street, New York 10014, N.Y.

Publication Office: 217 W. Jefferson Street, Bloomington, Illinois.

Manuscripts for publication (which should be accompanied by stamped, self-addressed envelope) and books for review should be sent to the Editor. The styling of manuscript should follow *The MLA Style Sheet* (obtainable from Modern Language Association, 6 Washington Sq. N., New York 10003, N.Y., 50 cents).

ETC.: A Review of General Semantics

OFFICIAL ORGAN OF THE INTERNATIONAL SOCIETY FOR GENERAL SEMANTICS, FOR THE ENCOURAGEMENT OF SCIENTIFIC RESEARCH AND THEORETICAL INQUIRY INTO NON-ARISTOTELIAN SYSTEMS AND GENERAL SEMANTICS. FOUR TIMES A YEAR.

•

VOL. XXIII, No. 3   SEPTEMBER 1966

CONTENTS

(cont.)

Drawings by GAIL McDONNELL

ETC.: A Review of General Semantics

Editor

S. I. HAYAKAWA
Professor of English, San Francisco State College

Associate Editors

ANATOL RAPOPORT
Professor of Mathematical Biology, University of Michigan

RICHARD DETTERING
Professor of English and Education, San Francisco State College

Assistant Editors

U. JAMES DOTSON
Assistant Professor of English, Sonoma State College

JOHN KEEL
Associate Professor of Art, San Francisco State College

DOROTHY MACDONALD
New York, N.Y.

Poetry Editor

ELIZABETH BARTLETT
Santa Barbara, California

Editorial Committee: SHEPARD A. INSEL, RICHARD P. MARSH, ROBERT E. MOGAR, EUGENE REBSTOCK, T. MIKE WALKER, San Francisco State College; STANLEY DIAMOND, LLOYD MORAIN, MARY MORAIN, BOB WANDERER, San Francisco; ARTHUR HASTINGS, Stanford University; ROBERT LUGTON, STATTON RICE, New York University.

Correspondents: THURMAN ARNOLD, Washington, D.C.; FRANCESCO BARONE, University of Pisa; ROGELIO DIAZ-GUERRERO, National University of Mexico; P. H. ESSER, Haarlem, Netherlands; LAWRENCE K. FRANK, Belmont, Mass.; GARRETT HARDIN, University of California at Santa Barbara; GÜNTHER KANDLER, Linguistic Institute of Bonn University; D. VUYSJE, International Society for Significs, Amsterdam; GEORGE A. LUNDBERG, University of Washington; A. H. MASLOW, Brandeis University; CHARLES MORRIS, University of Florida; TADATOSHI OKUBO, Japan Language Society, Tokyo; KARL R. POPPER, University of London; CARL R. ROGERS, Western Behavioral Science Institute, La Jolla, California; HENRY LEE SMITH, University of Buffalo.

294

REFLECTIONS ON
A VISIT TO WATTS

S. I. HAYAKAWA
BARRY A. GOODFIELD

[FOREWORD: *On Friday, May 27, 1966, Barry Goodfield, graduate student and part-time instructor at San Francisco State College, went to visit the Watts area of Los Angeles. The decision to go was the result, first, of Goodfield's concern with the possibility that there could be a repetition in Watts of the disturbances of August 1965. Secondly, it seemed to him, after working with Hayakawa both as student and teacher in training, that one who had studied general semantics might be able to take a fresh look at the Watts situation and perhaps contribute new insights.*

On Tuesday, May 24, Hayakawa and Goodfield had a conference in Sacramento with William Becker, Secretary to the Governor on Human Relations, to explain Goodfield's plans. Mr. Becker gave Goodfield a letter of introduction to facilitate contacts in the Los Angeles area.

On Friday evening, Goodfield, at a meeting arranged by George Stanley, president of the Los Angeles Chapter of the International Society for General Semantics, met a small group of Negro civic leaders. (Goodfield is white.) During the next three days, he toured the Watts area; attended meetings; visited jails and detention centers; went on calls with police officers in a squad car for an entire evening; spent time in pool halls, coffee houses, and a gambling establishment, interviewing people as he went.

Although the paper represents the thinking of both authors, Goodfield bears principal responsibility for the two sections, "What People Said" and "The Communicative Deadlock: The Police and the Community" (pp. 306-315). Good-

295

field is 25 years old, an honors graduate of San Francisco State College, where he is now doing graduate work in clinical psychology. He has had a variety of work experiences, including a period as undercover agent for the California Bureau of Narcotics Enforcement.]

TELEVISION AND THE REVOLUTION
OF RISING EXPECTATIONS

ALTHOUGH the causes of any great social revolution are many and complex, the student of semantics will tend to look first for the part that communications play in any large social event. A revolution in patterns of communication is always far more important than is realized at the time. (Think of the changes in Europe that followed the invention of printing!) The great and revolutionary communications instrument of the present is television. To what extent has television contributed to crystallizing and fomenting those discontents which add up to the present Negro revolution?

Before the advent of radio and television, to be illiterate was to be cut off from the world. But today the illiterate and the poorly educated, whether in New York, Chicago, Mississippi, or Watts, can hear about and see people and events he formerly would have known nothing about. Electronic communication has brought the whole big startling world into the lives and imaginations of millions who would never have been able to discover it through reading.

Furthermore, American television is commercially sponsored; it finds its economic support and justification in helping to push and promote consumer goods of all kinds. Hence television is always friendly, always beckoning cheerfully to the viewer, always inviting and alluring: "*Won't* you try our new cake mix?" "What did *you* think of the governor's message to the legislature?" "Drop in and test-drive the new Buick!" "Here is the latest news from the United Nations."

The spokesmen of the advertising profession continue to tell us that the moral and economic justification of their activities is that they create wants and stimulate demand and thereby elevate the standard of living. I have little quarrel with this argument. Advertising and mass production are profoundly democratizing influences. They put standard, mass-produced goods into the hands of everybody. They tell everybody, "No matter how miserable your present condition, you *can* be as good as anybody else. You too can look attractive. You too can have a beautiful and spotless kitchen. You too can lead an exciting jet-set life by taking the wheel of a new Mustang. You can enjoy all the satisfactions of living in our lush and abundant consumption economy!"

Now imagine that you are a Negro teen-ager, to whom the television set, with messages such as the foregoing, has been his constant baby-sitter and companion ever since he can remember. All your life, the friendly, friendly television set has been saying to you, "You are an American. You are entitled to eat and drink and wear what other Americans eat and drink and wear. You must think about the same political and world problems that other Americans think about. You are a member of the national community of Americans."[1]

"Now we have television," said one angry young man interviewed in Watts, "and we can see the difference between the way whites live and the way we live." Throughout the United States, television is accelerating the Negro demand for rights and opportunities. Its effect is powerful, although unintended. Indeed, given the dynamics of the television medium, it cannot help stirring up discontent. That's what advertising is for. No criticism of commercial television is intended in saying that its basic idea is to make people dissatisfied with what they have. Television merely promotes more effectively than any other medium the dynamics of our high-consumption, mass-production, free-enterprise society, in which it is held that the creating and fulfilling of people's wants will continue to stimulate aspirations and therefore the general standard of living, which in turn will continue to spur our industrial productivity and our national well-being.

---

[1] If this sounds familiar to old subscribers, it is because some of these paragraphs have been published here before. See Hayakawa, "Communication: Interracial and International," *ETC.*, XX (1963), 395-410.

I should like to reject out of hand, therefore, despite its charming simplicity, the John Birch Society theory that the whole Negro civil rights revolution is a communist plot. On the contrary, it is the result of a capitalist plot on the part of General Motors, General Electric, and General Foods, aimed at all of us, whites and Negroes and everyone else, to make

us discontented with what we have, so that we all aspire to newer automobiles, more convenient appliances, lovelier hair, yummier desserts, and in general more satisfying and glamorous lives. The civil rights revolution is also the result of the propaganda of free enterprise, traceable back at least to Benjamin

Franklin, which says that in a free country like our own those who are willing to work and improve their situations in life are invited, indeed, encouraged to do so, because here we have no permanent barriers of caste or class to keep the oppressed forever in rags.

In short, television has had the startling and revolutionary effect of causing Negroes, including the lower class, to regard themselves as part of the culture and entitled to its benefits. It has sharply increased the Negro's sense of his own situation. Lower-class Negroes, led by advertising to want and demand more at the same time as they are shut off from jobs and opportunities, are caught in a frustrating "double-bind." One result of this double-bind was all too clear during the Watts riots of last August, which were characterized by large-scale looting of stores for television sets, shoes, clothing, luggage, and other expensive consumer goods.

SOCIETY cannot indefinitely keep the people of Watts or Harlem or South Side Chicago in such a double-bind—simultaneously inviting them to share the abundant life while keeping them from sharing it. What are the alternatives?

We can on a large scale make social changes: changes in hiring practices, labor union policies, transportation facilities, education and training, and residential patterns, so as to enable the Negro to work for and earn what the society so eagerly and persuasively tries to sell him.

Another alternative is to go through Watts, Harlem, and Chicago South Side and confiscate television sets. However, that's not such a good idea if the purpose is to prevent, rather than cause, further rioting.

THE CRISIS IN TRANSPORTATION

"EACH MONTH," said a recent issue of *Look* (June 28, 1966), "about 2000 Negroes push in from the South and East, crowding this wide circle of poor. Watts, the bubbling core, is a ghetto in a ghetto in a ghetto. It is a stopping place with no exit."

The sense of Watts being a place from which there is no

escape is not due simply to its geographical location. There are many areas farther away from downtown Los Angeles where people feel no such sense of isolation. But with only 14% of Watts families owning automobiles (as compared with over 50% elsewhere in Los Angeles) and with shockingly inadequate transportation, the people are really in a trap. *Look* states that "A round trip to the Douglas Aircraft plant in Santa Monica from 103rd and Central takes five buses, three fares, and two transfers. Cost, $1.46; time, three hours and 50 minutes. The General Motors plant in Van Nuys, 22 miles from Watts, takes four hours and 45 minutes, $1.76 round-trip fare."

The McCone Report, in one of its strongest sections, emphasized the urgent need for a low-priced public bus system to connect Watts to the world outside. The report clearly recognized that such transportation could not be provided within the framework of the four existing bus systems and their financial requirements and urged that a public subsidy be provided "to accomplish three purposes: reduce fares, purchase or condemn the multiple uncoordinated bus system, and provide system-wide transfers. We believe that such a subsidy is justified because of public necessity and convenience, and therefore we have no hesitation in recommending it."[2]

A year after the riots and eight months after the publication of the report, little had been done to alleviate the sense of entrapment felt by the citizens of Watts. An experimental east-west bus line was started on July 5 on Century Boulevard; it seems to have met with instant acceptance. Governor Brown has obtained an emergency federal transportation grant to provide service to connect Watts with employment opportunities— a service which will be begun shortly. However, in the absence of local and municipal initiative, remedial action on the transportation problems of Watts has been slow. Why is society so often slow to act, even when everyone agrees that action is necessary?

---

[2] *Violence in the City: An End or a Beginning?* A Report by the Governor's Commission on the Los Angeles Riots [John A. McCone, Chairman], December 2, 1965.

THERE ARE two kinds of *can'ts*: the first refers to physical impossibility, as in, "We *can't* send a passenger rocket to the moon." This kind of *can't* is relatively easy to overcome; many of yesterday's *can'ts* are today's routines, like aviation or television. The more difficult kind of *can't* is the social impossibility, where the barriers are not brute physical facts, but social customs, rules, and regulations: "You *can't* drive without a driver's license," "We *can't* provide dental care for relief clients," "We *can't* provide buses for the people of Watts."

The social *can'ts* that stand in the way of urgent tasks are many. They involve all the institutions of a society: its statutes and laws, insurance regulations, obligations to banks and mortgage companies, union regulations, licensing requirements, and all kinds of contracts and agreements that constitute such a dense network of musts that nothing can be altered, nothing can even be accelerated.

Perhaps the most dramatic thing about human behavior is how many problems which are insoluble for institutional reasons are solved the moment a war breaks out. War is an institution, the demands of which take precedence over almost all

other demands. Before World War II, it would have been "impossible" to send the slum children of London to the country for the sake of their health. But when the air raids on London began, the evacuation of all the children took place over a weekend.

The problem of providing adequate bus transportation for

Watts is not a huge task for a city the size of Los Angeles. There is no shortage of materials, equipment, or labor. Imagine how it would relieve the pressures on Watts if there were adequate low-cost bus service to downtown Los Angeles. Imagine the boost to employment, the spur to ambition for all young people, the decrease of pressure on the police department, the change in the climate! The cost would be nothing compared to the gains. Yet so little is done.

One of the lessons of war is that the rigidity of social customs and institutions is not an insuperable barrier to action *if the emergency is great enough.* The emergencies of war are clear enough to all, but the emergencies of peace, the effect of slow strangulation by an accumulation of maladjustments, must be recognized by those in a position to know, then defined and acted upon. The tragedy of Watts is that not enough people in Los Angeles seem to know or care.

THE NEGRO AND CURRENT POLITICS

THE OUTLOOK for Negroes in California, from a political point of view, is cause for deep concern. There is little doubt that the "white backlash" has set in, especially in Southern California, where powerful conservative tendencies have emerged in the June primaries in both the Republican and Democratic parties. Ronald Reagan and Mayor Yorty, neither of whom have said anything to give the Watts Negro a shred of hope for anything better in his future, made better-than-expected showings.

Throughout the white world, there has been a long-standing tradition of trying to make Negro problems disappear. The middle and upper classes have done this by moving to the suburbs, drawing up housing restrictions against minority groups, and shutting their eyes. Working men, in many cases, have managed to accomplish the same thing by drawing up "grandfather clauses," limited apprenticeship programs, and elaborate evasive devices to keep Negroes out of their unions. One effect of the civil rights demonstrations, including the Watts riots (their impact was assured by mass television news coverage), has been, especially in California, to disturb profoundly the complacency of those whites who have thus shielded themselves from the problem of the American Negro. To those so disturbed, the promises of "law and order," especially when unaccompanied by any positive programs of social reconstruction such as would make law and order easier to attain, sound attractively reassuring. Throughout the propaganda of conservative resurgence is the appeal to nostalgia, to the desire for the restoration of an imagined *status quo ante*, before "communists" and "agitators" began stirring the Negroes up.

OF COURSE this conservative resurgence derives much inspiration from the Radical Right, which appears with greatest numbers and virulence in areas where social change is fastest, and where there are therefore, the greatest proportion of frightened people. Milton Rokeach, the social psychologist, has said that fearful and closed-minded people are characterized by the inability to see differences among ideas they disapprove of. For example if they dislike Democrats, liberal Republicans, communists, rock-and-roll musicians, atheists, and those who would fluoridate the water supply, they are able to say, apparently quite sincerely, that all these different people are communists or communist-led dupes. It is through this mechanism that people of the Radical Right are able to believe that the entire civil rights revolution is a communist plot.

Uneasiness about Negro demands becomes vaguely tied in with other uneasiness about the changing world—urban congestion, economic conditions, the pre-eminence of the Jews, international tensions, or whatever. And to many, a program of, if not repealing the 20th century, at least stopping it dead in its tracks, seems increasingly attractive. If such a program is approved by majority of voters, the prospects for all the poor and the disadvantaged of California are bleak indeed.

PERHAPS even more threatening to the Negro cause are certain elements in the New Left who present themselves as friends of the Negro. Granted that the New Left includes many who have dedicated themselves wholeheartedly and courageously to the Negro cause, it also includes those to whom the Negro is merely a convenient instrument with which to beat the "power structure" over the head.

At the moment the target of this segment of the New Left is the U.S. policy in Vietnam. Negroes have long protested their being "used" by business men, preachers, and politicians who profess an interest in the Negro cause only to advance their own schemes. Nowhere is this callous "using" of Negroes so apparent as in the behavior of such New Left leaders as Robert Scheer, who, in his determination to harrass and humiliate the national administration, vilifies all who do not fully agree with him on the war issue, regardless of their records of dedication and accomplishment on behalf of minority rights and opportunities.

SCHEER has publicly expressed his willingness to run as an independent and split the Democratic vote on the Vietnam issue. The fact that such an action would help to throw the election to a right-wing Republican, in place of the strong champion of minority groups and liberal causes, the incumbent Jeffery Cohelan, disturbs Scheer not at all. Such a tactic, if successful, would leave the large minority-group populations of Berkeley and Oakland with no effective representation. As Steven Kelman says in *Harper's* in a related connection (June 1966), "If you don't follow this logic, you've never played checkers with someone who knocks the board over when he starts losing."

The New Republic (June 4, 1966) carried an article on "Anti-Vietnam Politics" by Andrew Kopkind, which was generously quoted in political advertisements for Scheer. A sentence in this article reflects starkly and simply the position of Scheer's supporters on Negro welfare:

"Many in the [Scheer] campaign think that the ghetto is the logical place to start in *a campaign to change foreign policy*." (Italics added.)

In other words, the New Left campaign is admittedly not in behalf of the Negro at all. It is rather an attempt to use the disadvantaged Negro as an instrument with which to embarrass and discredit a national administration which, in civil rights legislation, education, voting rights, and the creation of economic opportunities, has done more for the Negro in three years than *any* previous administration has ever done in a comparable period. The campaign is also directed against a state administration which has taken more actions and passed more legislation to insure equal justice for the Negro, the Mexican-American, the Oriental, and other minorities than any administration in the history of California.

IN ANOTHER respect, the attitudes of the New Left in general to problems of power appear to be of little help to the Negro cause. The almost universal use of the expression "power structure" as an invective reveals a curious ambivalence: members of the New Left have a sweeping distrust of power when exercised by others; they also want power to disrupt the powerful; but most of all they do not want power that is accompanied by responsibility.

Power in America is always limited and shared power, exerted by alliances and coalitions of political parties, business groups, churches, unions, minority blocs, and the like. New Left leaders adroitly escape power (and therefore responsibility) by refusing to enter into alliances or coalitions, which they term "making deals" and "selling out." Standing on their ideological purity, they prefer the blazing rhetoric of moral denunciation to the give-and-take and the hemming-and-hawing of practical negotiation—for jobs, for better schools, for housing, for political support.

From the New Left, therefore, Negroes can expect nothing: not money, nor power, nor jobs, nor better schools, nor housing, nor political leverage.

The only hope for minorities, including the Negroes of Watts, lies in the broad center of both major parties—in those whose minds are neither in an imaginary past nor a visionary future, but in the realities of the present—in those who in the pragmatic, commonsense tradition of American life, will continue to hammer out the agreements and accommodations that we all must make to live together in peace and progress.

WHAT PEOPLE SAID
(Goodfield)

During my interviews with the people and police in Watts, I repeatedly asked a number of set questions. The following are the questions and a fair sample of the answers received:

QUESTION: *What is the main problem in Watts?*

ANSWERS (from Negroes):

"Quit playing political football. Start putting money into Watts. We need to give work to the people in Watts instead of giving all the jobs to white middle-class people."

"Before we didn't know any better, but now we got cats from the colleges and universities to tell what we need and to show us how to get it. That's one of the reasons we're in revolt."

"We've got TV also, and we are now aware of the big difference between the way the whites and the blacks live."

"We are powerless. The only power we have is the power to disrupt."

"Negroes must control their political and economic lives."

"Whites don't really care about us. They feel more secure with the police intimidating us."

"When all the kids down south got beat up—everyone saw it on television—they said, isn't that too bad. But the next day when some cat bombed a supermarket, the cops came running. They only care when business suffers."

ANSWERS (from white policemen):

"Negroes have no respect for law and order."

"The main problem in the Watts area is one of re-educating Negroes. They have no morals or values."

"Most Negroes down here [103rd St. area] are dope-peddlers, whores, pimps, drunks, and gamblers."

COMMENT:

From Negroes, by far the greatest number of answers to this question mentioned the Police Department as being, in one way or another, the "main problem." These answers will therefore be presented in a separate section.

QUESTION: *What is your opinion of the police department?*

ANSWERS (from Negroes):

"What can be done to reduce tensions here? Get the police to stop beating us up, right now!"

"The way to solve the problem is to leave us alone. We need someone to protect us from the police."

"Too many police officers come from the South and bring Southern white attitudes with them."

"They shouldn't assign so many rookie policemen to Watts."

"There should be more Negroes on the police force." (Although this suggestion was made several times, it was also disputed by a few, who felt that Negro police would, in order to prove themselves, be even tougher on Negro suspects than whites.)

"Police try to stir up trouble between Negroes and Mexicans so that they will kill each other off."

"The police commission is not doing its job. They have the power to bring about changes, but they do not. They are not sensitive to needs and problems of Negroes. They get their information from police officials instead of from the people."

"The white officer often fears the Negro, and this fear causes him to make inappropriate responses to Negroes that they meet daily."

"Police should be given regular psychiatric examinations."

"If you [Goodfield] go on a tour with the police and want to be at ease with them, you'd better use the word 'nigger' three or four times, right from the start."

"The frequent shifting around of prisoners, delays in booking, so that suspects are not able to get in touch with relatives or lawyers, may not be intended to deprive them of their rights; they may simply be a problem of regulations in the police department. These regulations should be reviewed." (Councilman Bradley)

"Police are too quick to issue traffic tickets in the Watts area. This makes for difficulty in licensing drivers and getting insurance. There should be a moratorium on excessive ticketing."

"Police must stop both physical and verbal brutality. Stop calling our women 'gal.' Stop insulting us. Treat us with the dignity and respect we are entitled to."

"Go to Firestone jail where they have a cold concrete bench for a bed and an air-conditioner overhead. When a Negro asks to have the air-conditioner turned off, the policeman says, 'Leave it on. It cuts down the smell.' "

"Negroes are not being responsible citizens. I am all for the police department. I think they are great." (Negro woman)

"Transfer from the 77th division all officers who are known to have had difficulties with Negroes."

"People should have a stake in their community. This can't be done without a change in the police."

"Police and Negroes are in a state of armed truce."

"Governor Brown should come and find out why police are allowed to operate as they do."

COMMENT:

Included in the comments on the police was much criticism of Chief Parker (since deceased). Most thought that he was a good administrator, but poor in human relations and human understanding. There were certain incongruities between words and deeds in my limited observations of police during the evening of May 28. Police at 77th Division Station said prisoners are entitled to six phone calls (to relatives, lawyer, etc.). It turned out that prisoners were not informed of this right "because there is only one telephone and it would be tied up too much." Again, it was explained to me that when a police call involved only a domestic quarrel, the police did not carry their shotguns; when we arrived on such a call, I saw a policeman running in with a shotgun in his hand.

On the other hand, I also saw cases of outstanding courtesy. For example, in the treatment of a drunken driving suspect, two officers, speaking in a polite and dignified way, explained to the suspect his rights before giving him a sobriety test (which he took and passed).

QUESTION: *What are the most pressing economic problems?*

ANSWERS:

"The most serious barrier to economic betterment is the lack of adequate public transportation. This first of all discourages industries from locating in Watts. People from this area spend as much as four hours getting to and from their jobs in downtown Los Angeles. This naturally prevents many from going out to seek jobs downtown."

"There is great difficulty in getting insurance, and therefore loans and financing for homes and businesses in Watts."

"Gambling takes millions out of this community. The three principal gambling operations in the area are chartered by the State of California as 'charitable organizations.' "

"Negroes have great difficulty getting into unions because of the 'grandfather clause.' Nevertheless, many belong to unions, pay their dues, but get little employment, since the jobs that turn up are said to be 'outside their [union] district.' "

"Whites should stop trying to soothe their conscience by spreading a thin layer of money over the Negro community. It isn't doing any good. It just shows us that they are trying to pacify us again."

"The poverty program is a farce. . . . The poverty program is a failure so far."

"There is great apathy among the school children, a high dropout rate in Jordan High School, and more than 300 teachers attempting to transfer out of Watts because of the tensions. We don't know what we are going to do to get more teachers."

"People who do not identify with the Negro community have been handling the poverty programs."

COMMENT:

Special bitterness is felt about the fact that in the little reconstruction that has been done since the riots, white trade-unionists are being employed to the almost total exclusion of Negro workers. It is also widely felt that Negroes may no longer have any economic function because of the advent of automation.

QUESTION: *Can communication between police and community be improved?*

ANSWERS:

"Do you think these guys really want to talk? I'm nineteen, man. Look at my hands. When I was fourteen I was handcuffed and hung up over a door in a police station. Don't tell me about these guys being nice and wanting to talk."

"Police should stop dealing with Watts as a foreign country." (Negro minister)

"We should have open seminars that anybody could attend, including Black Nationalists or any other organization, in conjunction with police officers. Negroes could get more face-to-face individual contact and learn that policeman are not all alike. Police could also learn that Negroes have morals and values and possibly have more things in common with policemen than differences." (Negro community relations officers)

"They might use role-playing techniques in human relations courses for new officers." (Councilman Bradley)

"If you want to talk to us, don't talk to ministers." (Black nationalist)

"If we had a fifteen-minute program giving the week's news from the Negro's point of view, it would reduce some of the tension. The Negro would have an opportunity to express his feelings about the situation he is experiencing."

"People like Joe Pine from KLAC cause a great deal of the problem. This is the fellow who [during the riots] pulled a revolver and said 'I've got mine. Do you have your gun?' "

"The mass media need much more self-policing to stop irrational and irresponsible broadcasting. Some newspapers also tend to sensationalism."

"Positive attempts on the part of police to improve community relations [e.g., sponsoring scout troops, etc.] should be better publicized."

"The Watts riots brought us international attention. That's the only way we can get them to listen to us." (Black nationalist)

"Governor Brown should come down to the Watts area and talk with us. The fact that he came last August proves he responds only to power. We are tired of speaking with Mickey Mouse and Donald Duck. We want to talk to Disney."

COMMENT:

As is clear from the foregoing, many (if not most) Negroes, and especially Black Nationalists, believe that communication with whites, especially police, is impossible. Many police officers seem to feel that communication with Negroes (except to order or direct them) is unnecessary. Saturday night at Watts Happening, two police officers and I met with some fifteen Black Nationalists, who were extremely truculent and defensive. One expressed willingness to fight and die. I asked if he was willing to talk rather than die. He said "We've been ready to talk all along." I asked Sergeant Allison if the police were ready to talk. He indicated they had always been willing. So I asked both, when? when? when? until they finally arranged a meeting for 8:30 Monday night.

Both sides exhibited a psychological condition extremely common under conditions of communicative deadlock. Each side believed in its own willingness to communicate. Each regarded the lack of communication as due to moral shortcomings of the other.

THE COMMUNICATIVE DEADLOCK:
THE POLICE AND THE COMMUNITY
(Goodfield)

THE STATEMENTS on the foregoing pages, gathered from an unsystematic selection of Negro and white civilians and police officers, are admittedly not fully representative of prevailing opinion in the Watts area. Nevertheless, one inescapable conclusion is that the major obstacle blocking the reduction of tensions is the lack of communication between the police and the Negro community.

The situation of communicative deadlock in Watts follows the classic pattern. Each "side," because of past misunderstandings and unfortunate experiences, has made inferences, hostile judgments, and generalizations about the other. Enough people on both sides are sufficiently anxious and defensive to have adopted group opinions, group attitudes, group ways of behaving toward the other side. Each assumes that the "other side" is unwilling to communicate, or, if willing, is so blinded by prejudice or ignorance as to be inaccessible to reason. "There's no use talking with people like that!"

The Los Angeles Police Department—specifically the 77th Division—appears genuinely concerned with relieving the tension and promoting better relations with the Negro community. However, the police assessment of the problem of the Watts area and the solutions proposed appear to be somewhat inflexible and not subject to modification through discussion and negotiation with the Negro community. This inflexibility appears to stem from the conviction on the part of police that they "know the best way to handle the situation." Many police officers in the 77th Division talk as if their perceptions of the problems and difficulties of the Watts area *are* the factual realities of the situation. Regardless of the validity of their perceptions, the way in which they are held serves to place an adverse value-judgment on any communication or new information that does not fit in with their preconceptions. There is the Negro's perception of the situation, and there is the police, or correct, perception. Judging from the comments of police officers, the tendency towards such a two-valued orientation is deeply rooted in the 77th Division.

A SIMILAR two-valued outlook characterizes many individuals and leaders among the Negroes. Negroes usually feel that they know, *really* know, the actualities of the situation, while police perceptions are distorted by prejudice, ignorance, and malevolence. Almost all Negroes in the Watts area are convinced that they are subjected to unjust harrassment by the police: as one Negro minister said, they are tired of being treated like an occupied country. Many are eager to tell their personal stories of mistreatment by the police. Another informant said, "Everyone who is getting into trouble with the police is not a criminal. Many are law-abiding and are just trying to stand up for their rights and help their community." With widespread feelings of this kind, it is but a short step, given a prevailing two-valued orientation, to feeling that the *total* problem in the Watts area is police hostility against the people living there.

The two-valued orientation is most dangerous in the "extreme" Negro organizations, i.e., those organizations that are generally identified with the Black Nationalist movement. The positive side of Black Nationalism is the serious attempt to instill pride of race and self-respect into the discouraged and defeated, especially through the teaching of Negro (Afro-American) history. The negative side is the tremendous sense of grievance against whites as being responsible for almost everything that ails the Negro community. Nationalists believe that they alone understand and are willing to confront the "true nature" of white people. White people are not to be trusted; they may appear sincere on the surface, but they are only attempting to manipulate the black man for their own gain, as they have done for the past three hundred years. With such a view, Nationalists are singularly deaf to communications,

not only from whites, but also from Negroes holding different views.

There are rigidities of attitude on both sides. Many police officers seem to have real difficulty in seeing Negroes as individuals. When Negroes charge that they are frequently detained, questioned, and searched without cause just because they are Negroes, the reason is not far to seek. As one officer said, "The whole problem stems from the fact that Negroes have no values or morals." To officers who hold such a view, every Negro is by definition a suspect and *should* be detained, questioned, and searched, because even if he hasn't done anything wrong yet, he is likely to at any moment. The repeated Negro demand that they be treated "with the respect to which they are entitled" appears to be simply a demand that they not be treated as suspects when a white person, under similar circumstances, would not be so treated.

ON BOTH SIDES rigidities of attitude result in the ignoring of differences that occur over a period of time. It is clear that since the riots of August 1965, there has been careful, and to some degree effective, retraining of police officers in the direction of greater thoughtfulness and courtesy, as well as greater circumspectness of behavior in order not to justify charges of "police brutality." However, many Negroes, reacting to how the police used to behave rather than to how they are trying now to behave, often act in such a way as to restimulate in the police their former reactions.

In other words, attitudes on both sides operate as "self-fulfilling prophecies." The paranoiac who expects everyone to be his enemy and acts on that expectation makes his belief come true; he soon hasn't a friend in the world. The happy child in the park, who smiles at everyone in the expectation of friendliness, extracts a smile even from the surliest passer-by. Both Negroes and policemen, by expecting hostile behavior from each other, unwittingly evoke in each other exactly the kind of actions they fear. For example, one officer said about an establishment said to be a headquarters of the Black Nationalist movement, "I've never been in there. Frankly, I'm afraid to go in there because I know the way they would react to me." Perhaps his fears are justified.[3] However, how will he act if it ever becomes necessary for him to enter those premises in the line of duty? His preconceptions will probably affect profoundly the way he behaves—and therefore the way he is received.

The greatest danger confronting Watts is the operation of this kind of self-fulfilling prophecy. If Negroes continue to expect trouble from the police, and if police continue to expect trouble from Negroes of the community, their very expectations will trigger dangerous incidents. And those incidents are all too likely to become magnified, since policemen, expecting more trouble, will call more cars, and spectators, expecting more "police injustice," will gather in larger numbers. It has happened before. It can happen again, especially because the community's sense of pride and the Negroes' determination to have a hand in the shaping of their own destinies have become more clearly articulated since August 1965.

A Working Hypothesis:
"Communication Is Possible"

A NUMBER of meetings have taken place in Watts since Barry Goodfield was there the week-end of May 27-30. During the confrontation at Watts Happening on Saturday night, May 28, at which both police and Black Nationalists expressed willingness to communicate, Goodfield insisted upon their setting a date for another meeting immediately. The next evening an open meeting between representatives of the two groups (including Lieutenant Beeson) took place, apparently the first of its kind ever held.

Negro conservatives-to-moderates and red-hot militants, having shouted at each other and at Goodfield at the meeting

---

[3] In this case, the officer's fears were quite unjustified. Goodfield and I have both visited the place and were received cordially. When I was there, some young people were rehearsing a play; others were practicing Afro-Cuban dances; and a creative writing group in a corner was reading their verses to each other. S.I.H.

at Operation Bootstrap on Sunday, May 28, have been meeting together to form the (Temporary) Alliance of Local Organizations—having learned that *vis-à-vis* the police they have a problem in common (although they agree about practically nothing else). Mrs. Tiger Slavik of Newsworthies Unlimited (a volunteer public relations agency devoted to sending out positive news about Watts) reports that Negro militants have come to her since the Goodfield visit to ask for help in communicating with whites. Louis Gothard of BLOOD (Brotherhood of Local Organizations for Opportunities and Development), having come to believe that communication is possible, asked for a hearing before the Police Commission, which granted him one.

The Police Commission hearing was well covered by press, radio, and television. Afterwards, Ron Karenga of US, a nationalist group, was interviewed by both NBC and CBS, and he had the satisfaction of seeing himself on television, his interviews uncut. The reaction of the Police Commission to Gothard's demands on behalf of the Watts community was also thoroughly reported by the media. The feeling expressed earlier by members of the community that the media never pay attention to Negroes' views has at least been partly mitigated.

Robert Brock and H. A. Jamal, who regard themselves as militants, have been added to Tiger Slavik's "Truth Squad," a group of speakers who meet with church, civic, social, and fraternal groups to talk and answer questions about the Negro community. Watts speakers, along with representatives of the Mexican-American community, have had the opportunity of presenting their case before a large meeting of ministers constituting the Commission on Church and Race of the Southern California Council of Churches. Admittedly, these few meetings and opportunities for contact do not add up to much, because Watts is a very large place; nevertheless, they indicate a change of direction from the steady deterioration of relations described by almost all informants. Several channels of communication have been opened that had not existed before, not only between whites and Negroes, but also between groups of Negroes.

WHY was Goodfield able to act as a catalyst, initiating interaction between those who had firmly believed in the impossibility of mutual communication? He has many personal qualities of energy, curiosity, courage, and previous experience in investigation and interrogation. However, these alone do not explain the outcome, because many others with, no doubt, equal capacities and certainly with greater experience in community relations have been working in Watts for a long time without getting comparable results. Mrs. Slavik quite explicitly says that Goodfield, during his very short visit, made a real difference to a number of people.

What Goodfield brought to the situation, it seems to me, is the unique faith of the general semanticist, namely, that whenever human beings are involved, *communication is possible.* This doesn't sound like much of a principle until it is

seen in the context of customary behavior. Negroes say about policemen, police say about Negroes, moderates say about extremists and extremists about moderates—indeed, *every*body says about *some*body—"There is no use trying to talk to people like that! They won't listen. They wouldn't understand if they did listen!"

However, the statement, "Communication is impossible,"

is rarely if ever based on experience in trying to communicate. Usually, it is both an inference about the character of the other fellow, and a judgment upon him. It is, as Goodfield remarked, a closed mind calling another mind closed. For example, it was said about the meeting planned for Sunday afternoon at Operation Bootstrap that the Black Nationalists would not come and that it wouldn't do any good to invite them. Nevertheless, Goodfield insisted that they be invited—and 25 were invited, of whom 23 came. In short, the statement, "Communication is impossible," becomes a self-fulfilling prophecy. One ceases to try—and the resulting non-communication fulfills the prophecy.

BUT the general semanticist's belief, "Communication *is* possible," also acts as a self-fulfilling prophecy. Goodfield simply refused to take anyone's word for it that communication was impossible. So to police officers and red-hot militants and everyone else, he kept putting the question, "OK, if you are willing to communicate, when are you going to start?"

The principle that communication is possible is perhaps the most important idea that general semanticists can contribute to a troubled Watts—and perhaps to a troubled world. To say that communication is impossible is to say in effect that only force can effectuate social change. To say that it is possible is to begin listening, with respect and interest and curiosity and patience to the other fellow's views, no matter how threatening or bizarre they may seem at first, until you begin to understand how he sees the world. When you begin to understand why he says what he says, your defenses begin to relax, because while he may still seem mistaken, he will no longer seem mad. And as the other fellow begins to realize that you are genuinely trying to understand his view, his defenses also relax, and real exchanges can begin.

It is not claimed that communication of itself will solve the problems of Watts. But it is clear that meaningful communication and the establishment of trust between the police and the citizens of Watts is a condition of further improvements and reforms of all kinds, including especially the formation of new community organs of self-help and mutual aid and the re-opening and establishing of businesses that the community so desperately needs.

Community leaders, police officials, patrolmen, and ordinary citizens can be taught how to work on the assumption that communication is possible. It would seem that a generous scattering of people so trained might effect a real change in the climate in Watts—or in any other community with similar problems. Such a change of climate would make possible, through meaningful dialogue, the solution of many community problems now deemed insoluble.

IN FACT, the climate is already changing. In the July 15, 1966, issue of *Life*, with cover headlines, "WATTS STILL SEETHING . . . Why the ghetto is close to flashpoint," there appeared a sensational 26-page story, "There's Still Hell to Pay in Watts," featuring pictures of violent action, close-ups of sullen Negroes faces, and rows of grim-faced, armed police-men. Angered by the incendiary character of this story, two Watts residents, Billy Tidwell, a social worker, and Stan Sand-ers, a Yale law student, decided to carry out a plan already maturing in their minds to show the world the positive side of Watts.

Working with the Jordan High School Alumni Associa-tion, of which they are members, and the Community Alert Patrol (originally formed to keep an eye on the police), they organized a Watts Festival for the weekend of August 12-14, on the anniversary of the riots, to celebrate "a year of progress." There were jazz concerts, a beauty contest, dance recitals, art shows, plays, a basketball exhibition (well-known professionals contributed their services) and educational displays. A vast amount of joyous energy was released in preparation for the festival, of which the high point was the parade, with Sargent Shriver flying in from Washington to act as grand marshal. Over ten thousand attended the festival, which attracted na-tional attention through newspapers and net works, enhancing community pride.

The festival committee discovered that unemployed youthful loiterers, most of them delinquents, threw themselves with great energy, enthusiasm, and intelligence into helping with the festival when called upon. This discovery led to the foundation of the Sons of Watts Improvement Association (SWIA), with a novel scheme for employing these youths in

programs of community protection (security patrols for school-children), of tidying up the community, of securing counseling and job training, and of *improving communication with the Los Angeles Police Department!*

The Watts community has internal resources that few outside have suspected.

MINORITY PROGRESS
IN CALIFORNIA

ONE PROBLEM of the poor is that they often do not know what help is available to them, how to seek employment, how to get on-the-job training, how to apply for state and community services. In response to this need, multiple-service centers were set up through state initiative in May and June, 1966 —one in East Los Angeles for a Mexican-American neighborhood, the other in Watts—the first of twelve such centers planned. At the one in Watts, the South Central Los Angeles State Service Center, various state and municipal departments (social welfare, legal aid, skill center, public assistance, etc.), representatives of federal and defense agencies, voluntary city-wide organizations (such as the Merit Employment Committee of the Management Council), are able to share problems with each other and coordinate their activities. Through the work of the Management Council, more than fifty large firms (Bank of America, Douglas Aircraft, Goodyear, J. C. Penney's, Sears, North American Aircraft, U.S. Rubber, Western Electric, to name only a few) have been interviewing prospects and hiring them.

The voluntary Willowbrook Job Corps (sewing classes, boat-building projects, etc.), Operation Bootstrap ("Learn, baby, learn"), and other organizations continue to build up skills and hope. Small businesses such as restaurants, automatic laundries, printing shops, and dry cleaners provide the continuing encouragement of modest success.

THE MULTIPLE-SERVICE center is, of course, only one of the ways in which action has been taken by the state to improve the situation in Watts and other troubled areas. Remedial actions of the past year were certainly accelerated by the Watts emergency. But they also occur in a context. In no state of the Union has there been more steady and active concern for civil rights and equality of opportunity in recent years than there has been in California. Fair employment was a major issue in Edmund G. Brown's 1958 campaign for the governorship and the first item on his legislative agenda for the 1959 session of the legislature. The Unruh Rights Act, which forbids discrimination in all business establishments, was also enacted in this session. The fair housing legislation of 1963, partially nullified by the passage of Proposition 14, which in turn was declared unconstitutional by the California Supreme Court, shows the continuing concern of the administration with this important issue.

Other civil rights gains have passed into the realm of the

matter-of-fact so completely that most people have forgotten that they are the result of specific decision and initiative on the part of the Brown administration. The ban on alien land ownership removed an injustice that was especially felt by the Chinese and Japanese, against whom it was originally directed. The law against intermarriage was rescinded. A commission to prevent discrimination in the hiring of teachers was created; it was later expanded to deal with the problems of *de facto* segregation. Non-citizens were enabled by law to apply for old age assistance. Panic selling, which contributed so much in the past to housing segregation, was prohibited. It was written into law that restrictive covenants are not enforceable. Compensatory education was pioneered in California two years before the United States Congress acted in this field.

Aside from legislation, a number of administrative actions were taken towards the equalization of opportunities for minorities. An ethnic census of civil service employees was taken in 1963 and 1964, and there has been a continuing aggressive program to recruit Mexican-Americans and Negroes to apply for and take examinations for civil service jobs. Nondiscrimination clauses have been inserted into every state contract except the smallest, not just in construction, but in purchase order services and leases as well. Every state office that deals with the public now has some Spanish-speaking staff, and some departments have created Mexican-Spanish-speaking civil service job classifications. California's program for increasing minority participation in apprenticeships became the model for the national efforts by the U.S. Department of Labor.

TRAINING for jobs is also an important area of minority concern. In this area, California leads the nation—in classes under the Manpower Development and Training Act (MDTA), in on-the-job apprenticeship programs (by July 1, 1966, there were 8000 on-the-job trainees enrolled), and in the opening of the new Skill Centers in East Los Angeles (Watts) and Oakland, equipped to train 5,000 people a year.

The state is pouring millions into special aid to schools in disadvantaged areas: to prevent dropouts, to reduce class size, to build new schools. California leads the world in creating opportunities for higher education. The rapid expansion of the University of California system, with new branches in Santa Cruz, Irvine, San Diego, and Riverside, has been accompanied by an aggressive program of recruiting students from the Negro and Mexican-American minorities. There has been an equally rapid expansion of the system of California State Colleges, while community colleges (an educational development pioneered by California) have been proliferating with unprecedented speed.

All these developments add up to an overwhelming fact, namely, that *a child born in California has a better chance of getting a college education than one born anywhere else in the world.* The opportunity is there also for the young people of Watts, with Compton College (a public, two-year institution) and California State College at Dominguez Hills (a four-year college opened in September 1966), in immediately adjacent districts.

FINAL THOUGHT

THERE are far worse fates than to be a Negro in Watts. The citizen of Watts has political representation, and he can learn to use his political power to better advantage as time goes on. He has millions of concerned allies, in and out of the government, who are putting into practice our professed creeds of equality of treatment and opportunity.

Most importantly, the Negro of Watts lives in a society of people many of whom have gone through some of his experiences. European peasants came to America burdened by poverty and illiteracy. There are few immigrant groups that did not confront prejudice, sometimes of a virulent kind. The victims of this prejudice were known as wops, hunkies, polacks, kikes, micks, and many other names not so printable. Most of the Negro's fellow-Americans know, either in their own generation or those of their parents or grandparents, some of the op-probrium that attaches to the outsider.

Being of Oriental extraction myself, I think of the Chinese of Gold Rush days, of how they were lynched for sport on Saturday nights by the Forty-Niners and their successors, so that the expression "a Chinaman's chance" came to be used to mean no chance at all. I think of the ugly expressions about the Japanese and Chinese used by the trade unionists and the "yellow peril" agitators in the early years of this century. I think of Hiram Johnson running successfully for governor of California as recently as 1924 on an anti-Oriental ticket. I think of the War Relocation, which I happily escaped, being a Chicagoan at the time. I think of the way the Chinese survived their initiation into the culture and became an honored group in the community of Californians. I think of the triumphant return of the Nisei soldiers after World War II, and of the fact that Japanese-Americans have experienced practically no racial discrimination since that time.

Furthermore, Watts is only a portion of the Negro community of Los Angeles. Outside this "ghetto in a ghetto in a ghetto," there are hundreds of thousands of Negroes working, going to school or teaching, making money, rooting for the Angels or the Dodgers, distinguishing themselves in sports, theater, business, and the professions, fully participating in the seething dynamic that is Southern California. There are still barriers to surmount, but these barriers have only the sanction of custom, not of law. America remains an open society—and nowhere is this openness more apparent than in California. To be a Negro in California is a far, far cry from being a black in South Africa.

SOMETIMES it seems to me that race prejudice in America is not as important as culture prejudice—prejudice against those of unfamiliar modes of behavior, language, and dress. There is a certain amount of class prejudice, but it is maintained with difficulty when today's singing star or United States senator is yesterday's slum child.

Basically, Negroes are victims of a caste system, which was

originated in the South after Reconstruction in order to avoid the social adjustments made necessary by the abolition of slavery. The victory of the South lies in the unconscious absorption by the rest of the nation of Southern caste attitudes towards the Negro. Nevertheless, caste remains so entirely foreign to American ideology that articles on the subject in encyclopedias (for example, the *Americana, Britannica,* and *World Book*) deal with the caste system in India—and never mention the situation of the American Negro! Hence, the same people who vehemently oppose open housing for Negroes (for what are clearly reasons of caste separation) are likely to deplore the Indian caste system and to espouse vehemently a completely equalitarian philosophy.

The American caste system, having no ideological foundations, is therefore neither reliable nor permanent. For this reason, no one in America is forever stuck in the slot in which he finds himself. If he can't get out of it himself, his children or grandchildren will. Many of the Okies that Steinbeck wrote about are the prosperous farmers and merchants who voted for Goldwater in '64 and in '66 grew apoplectic about the strikers of Delano. Things just don't stay put.

Perhaps that's why Negroes from the East and South keep coming to Watts anyway. To many, Watts looks like the end of hope. But to some, it continues to look like the first way-station to the Promised Land.

FOUR POEMS

A ROSE IS NOT A NAME

dear Gertrude:
a rose is not a rose
until it joins the mind in thought—
nor bee nor butterfly can pose
the object for our inner eye—
unseen, unknown, unsought.
one *learns* the rose,
sunsets and trees,
and that highway traffic *flows*—
then, if the patterns
tell the brain it *sees,*
the mind becomes aware it knows,
and, happily, invents the symbol, *rose.*

I say:
take the rose—
red, or yellow tea,
on bushes, in vases,
even in imaginary places.

I say:
take the rose—
Juliet's or Cummings'
Gertrude Stein's, or Burns',
take them, together, or in turns.

then tell me:
Did you use your nose,
or pen to grasp it?

did you use hand,
heart, or mind to clasp it?

I say:
drain your mind of words,
then inject roses—
and if your brain bleed
like your thorn-stuck thumb,
evict the mental thorns—
and stick them—
onto roses.

HARRY P. KROITOR

Bryan, Texas

TICKTACKTOE

When I became myself, I had
to say over and over, "give
your life to a straight line; cross
here and you lose, and if you stay,
you gain."

I didn't know once
what it meant to go forward.
So many lines were there to follow:
O's I made, and X's made
by others—not one connecting.

My infant son—it may have nothing
to do with this—my son reaches
and feels, where his legs meet, the line
he finds beyond his straight body.
He looks at me. He is fingering
the soft flesh. He doesn't know.

JOHN STEVENS WADE

Temple, Maine

OFFICE TEN A.M.

ah
matutinal attitude
like noodles
long and almost endless
winding 'round the fork
of work

yes
hangover
that hangar which
as you can plainly see
houses the darkly roar
of my indisposition

no
I didn't booze it up
and I don' wonna take a snooze
yawn yawn on a scratch pad
I'm playing with my mood
that's all

BOZENA NEMCOVA

Berkeley, California

SPAIN IN NOVEMBER

Riding behind the wood-burning locomotive
From the gardens of the coast to the kilns
Of Játiva, we saw the horizon proliferate
In wool spun from the black-faced sheep.
Cathedrals rose in air, houses and walls
Of towns the wind blew to smithereens
Before the wind died in the long grass.
We stopped at each station, installments
Of parleys with peasants over fruit, cheese,
The rolls called *bollitos*. Our hunger immense,

329

We devoured cactus or drank rivers of sand
Jolting when the train bucked, appeased
By sour wine and the hard thrust of air.
The gypsies of Villacañas played reed pipes.
At La Encina buzzards patrolled the fields.
The wounds of the Virgin at Mura bled anew
So that the blank wall ahead blushed for us,
For our innocence lost in the smoky tunnel,
And at Albacete the baggage-man resembled
Rey Alfonso, but there the dust rolled down
With the mountain cold, and a thin glow
Illumined paintings that lacked frames.
For a moment, we were stretched by memory.
The canvas reached to the farthest peak,
The brush spread like feathers from a hawk
To drop on the arid plain and stipple day.
But soon we gaped at a lesser landscape:
The pastures blooming with empty tins,
The roofs of factories riddled by sunset,
And at Alcazar the conductor came unsmiling
For our tickets, warning us of disaster.
Madrid! he called in somber tones. *Madrid?*
After the long journey and the steep ascent
Only licensed guides, beggars at church doors,
The blind statues of the Catholic kings.

LAWRENCE P. SPINGARN

INVOLUNTARY INSTITUTIONALIZATION:
Some Legal, Ethical, and Social Implications

EDWARD S. SULZER *

PEOPLE WHO ARE COMMITTED to institutions involuntarily are committed there on primarily social grounds.
That is, questions of science and medicine and psychiatry
which are often introduced in the involuntary institutionalization of an individual are in fact not real considerations. The
concept I propose is that mental illness (and there are many
terms used as synonyms or euphemisms) is not mental and
not an illness.

In the first place, mental illness is not mental; it is a problem of human behavior. In the second place, it is not an illness: It is essentially socially unacceptable behavior; that is,
behavior which, from the point of view of those people who
impinge on a person's life and environment, is undesirable;
behavior which is irritating, annoying, unpleasant, or, in some
cases, not of advantage to that person in everyday life.

This paper does not touch on the scientific aspects of involuntary institutionalization. It is restricted to the social, the
ethical, and the legal. The reason is that as a scientist, I do
not view the problems that we generally deal with in the treatment of the psychiatric patient, or the so-called mentally ill
individual, as essentially scientific today. These are questions
of ethics, morals, social and societal values, and law. Very
often, activities in the legal or social arenas are alleged to be
scientific or the products of some part of science. I suggest
that the allegation is false insofar as our treatment of the involuntary psychiatric patient is concerned.

* Rehabilitation Institute, Southern Illinois University, Carbondale.
Excerpts from an address before the National Convention of the
American Conference of Therapeutic Self Help Clubs, June 22, 1962.

What we do in the name of science is sometimes not scientific and, in fact, goes against the overwhelming evidence we find in the field as scientists. Usually, in science, we expect that the criterion for the labeling of anything or any person will allow us to differentiate the thing or person from anything else we deal with. In the field of mental illness, or the mentally disabled, this is not the case. The evidence today is against the hypothesis that there is any high degree of concordance among psychiatrists, psychologists, psychiatric social workers, and other people working in the field of mental health.

WHAT IS mental illness for one person in one society at one time is often not mental illness for another person in another society despite the fact that the behavior of the two individuals is highly similar or in fact identical. A recent case in one of our Southern states is a good example. A young Negro man who was applying to the law school at one of our Southern state universities was apprehended by the state police on the grounds that he was mentally ill. He felt that Negroes in his state should be treated as fairly as white people. This became the criterion for mental illness in the situation.

In a fairly well publicized case in the city of Chicago, two people—a married couple, immigrants to this country from Poland, refugees from Nazi persecution—were institutionalized, partly because they could not speak English very well. They had few friends in this country, having been here briefly, and they did not understand—nor was it explained to them—what they were doing in a courtroom. They were not provided with sufficient information about what was happening to them. They were institutionalized against their will and, unfortunately, institutionalization led to the death of one of them.

Other examples could be offered to demonstrate the fact that what we have today is not a system based upon science, but a system based on certain viewpoints people have socially and ethically. Some of these viewpoints have been established in our laws; they have become statutory or have become part of our common law or have become part of administrative procedure.

In a recent volume, Thomas Szasz, Professor of Psychiatry at the State University of New York, examines the problem of how mental illness came to be considered illness; that is, what brought it under the purview of medicine and, most particularly, psychiatry. In effect, he demonstrates how, to a large extent, this was a historical development based almost on accidental happenings. What we call mental illness could very well have become a matter of theological and religious concern, as it was in the Middle Ages. That is, a person was not mentally ill but was suddenly possessed by the devil. Historically, neurologists became interested in problems of behavioral

deviation and in people whose behavior was not socially accepted. As a result, it became a medical problem, particularly when a leading specialist of the time decided that behavioral deviation was an illness. This was a medical decision. Society at that time, particularly French and Austrian-German society, adopted this point of view. Some behaviors are sick and therefore a medical problem. From that acceptance developed the present-day specialty of psychiatry.

WHY IS THIS an ethical problem and, for many people— particularly clergymen—a moral or religious problem? In our society, as well as in other societies, we have developed our own ethical and moral codes which deem certain behavior desirable or good and other behavior undesirable, bad, or evil. In our culture there are many features of a person's behavior which are viewed as undesirable. When a man's behavior is viewed as undesirable, and when people in his surroundings find it difficult to explain to themselves why his behavior is what it is, he is very likely to end up with the label "mentally ill." It generally requires at least these two characteristics: first, the behavior is viewed by some person or persons as undesirable; second, it is difficult to understand. A recent case in New York City can demonstrate this. A Negro woman attacked the Reverend Martin Luther King, the leader of a variety of movements in the South to increase the speed of integration. This woman was a Negro. When she attacked Dr. King, she was immediately apprehended, accused, and later convicted of having a mental illness.

Let us assume for the moment, however, a hypothetical case in which it was a Southern white woman who had attacked Dr. King. Would she too have been considered mentally ill? I doubt it. I think this would have been seen as politically or socially motivated action which was criminal in its intention and should be treated as a crime. But since it was difficult to understand why a Negro woman should attack a Negro minister who had been so important in the Negro's effort to obtain integration and equality in the South, people said, "This must be a crazy act. How else can we explain it?" Therefore, this woman was sent to Bellevue Hospital and it was alleged that she was mentally ill.

Now, one might ask, Is it not better for a person to be thought of as mentally ill in our society than to be thought of as a criminal? I would raise very serious doubts about that. In criminal law in this country, there are many safeguards afforded the individual who is accused of committing a crime. On the whole, the very same safeguards are *not* afforded to the person accused of being mentally ill. In our criminal courts, a person is generally deemed to be innocent until proven guilty. When a person is accused of being mentally ill, the situation is reversed. Generally, the burden of proof falls on other people; they must demonstrate the presence or probable presence of something. But it becomes the burden of the accused person to demonstrate that he is *innocent* of the charge of mental illness. Since this cannot be established in a scientific sense, it falls into the legal, social, and ethical areas for demonstration of the absence or presence of something called mental illness. It is not a scientific enterprise.

WHAT ABOUT the provisions made to safeguard individuals who are accused of being mentally ill? What happened when a person is so accused, and how does this compare to the situation in which the same person might be accused of a criminal act?

In this country when it comes to the accusation of mental illness and the requirements necessary to institutionalize involuntarily, we find that thirty-seven of our fifty states require some form or have some form of judicial hospitalization. On what basis may the court decide which person may be institutionalized involuntarily?

In five states the sole criterion in the law is that a person is dangerous to himself or others. The prediction of this, scientifically, is a most awkward business; if one looks at the data that we have accumulated for several decades both in this country and in other countries we find that this is a peculiar requirement because one cannot successfully predict either for individuals or for groups whether a man will be a danger to himself or to others. If anything, a psychiatric patient is demonstrably less dangerous to himself and to society than members of many other groups which are not psychiatrically labeled.

Twelve states say that a person may be institutionalized if he is a danger to himself or to others and also needs treatment. Presumably we have forms of treatments which are efficacious for the psychiatric patient who is ill. Again, we would have to fly in the face of scientific evidence. If anything, the institutions to which people are committed involuntarily probably do not help the person any more than he would be helped were he not hospitalized. In fact, the evidence most recently published suggests that a person is often better off outside an institution than he is inside.

Seven states in our country have only the requirement that the person require treatment to be hospitalized. He does not have to be dangerous to himself or to others. In one state, we have the most honest, though strange, statute regarding hospitalization. The state is Massachusetts. This state says, essentially, in its statutes, "any social nonconformity will lead to involuntarily institutionalization, and this may be the only basis." I say this is an honest statute because it recognizes what is implicit in the statutes of all other states; that is, that it is social nonconformity that introduces people into the court and later into a hospital against their will.

In five states, there are no statutory requirements. That is, it is entirely up to the judge in the particular court assigned the task to decide, without the guide of statutory law, whether a person should be institutionalized. This is what we call judicial hospitalization. But there are also other forms—admin-

istrative and medical. In nineteen states of this country any citizen of the state may initiate proceedings in a court of this state to get any other citizen of the state involuntarily institutionalized. In other words, if your neighbor, friend, relative, spouse, child, or parent wishes to institute proceedings, he may do so; the law does not require that he demonstrate the presence or absence of any phenomenon called mental illness. It also does not require that the complainant demonstrate that he will not benefit from the accused's institutionalization. In many cases the spouse, parent, or child benefits from the hospitalization of the relative.

In eleven states, when a person applies for the commitment of another citizen, a physician must be brought in to the affair. A physician must certify that, in his opinion, such an action is called for. In four additional states, two physicians must be called into action to bring the person into the hospital against his will.

NOW WHAT HAPPENS when John Jones, Mary Jones, John Doe, Mary Doe, is accused of being mentally ill and requiring hospitalization? Let's take a general case here that differs slightly from state to state. The person is accused of being mentally ill and requiring hospitalization, and a variety of proceedings may now occur. Ordinarily, in criminal law, were a person accused of committing a crime he would immediately, of course, have the right to communicate with counsel, an attorney of his own choosing—or, if he were indigent, an attorney assigned by the court. What happens to the person accused of being psychiatrically or mentally ill? In only *seven* of our fifty states does a person accused of being mentally ill have the unrestricted right to counsel and to communicate freely with counsel. Forty-three states do *not* provide this safeguard.

In only nineteen of the fifty states is it required that the person who is accused of being mentally ill must be given notice that he is so accused, and that there will be a hearing, and that there may be physicians involved, and that there will be a judicial determination, and that he might end up in the hospital against his will for an indeterminate period. Again, only nineteen states require that the person be informed.

Now, one would imagine that, if someone's life is going to be dealt with in this fashion, not only should he know about it, but he should be present when these decisions are being made. After all, it is mandatory in Anglo-Saxon countries that a person be present if he is being charged with and being tried for a crime. Yet in only ten states of the United States is the patient required to be in attendance. In other words, forty of our states say, "Well, we are not going to require that the person accused and tried be present." Only nineteen states require that he be told, and of those nineteen, only ten require that he be there. Twelve states say to the patient, "Well, we'll let you into the hearing if you demand it and *if* the court accepts this demand as reasonable."

One would expect that a number of legal safeguards would have been introduced in all of our fifty states, but some very interesting things have happened in this regard. Of the fifty states, only half require that the proceedings take place in a courtroom or in any other location that is usually used for judicial hearings or judicial decisions. In other words, twenty-five states authorize that a hearing may be held outside of a courtroom in any informal situation as may be deemed desirable by the court. Hearings have been held everywhere—including, in one case, a lavatory. This means that often there is no legal record kept of the proceedings. A judgment may be entered without much of a record. Problems are dealt with in a criminal proceeding by an open evaluation of the issues. This cannot be accomplished in such an informal, almost hit-or-miss procedure.

One would also expect that, if social non-conformity is the reason a person is institutionalized, a group of his peers should have some evaluative role in determining whether his behavior is truly nonconforming or unacceptable to the public. In criminal trials, we accept the idea that a jury of a man's peers may be introduced. No state of this country requires a jury trial for the person accused of mental illness. Ten states permit it on the demand of the patient; and, of those ten, three require that the court agree to it.

THE United States Supreme Court has ruled that Article 3 of the United States Constitution does not guarantee the right of trial by jury in state courts in civil trials. This includes the adjudication of mental illness, insanity, or involuntary institutionalization. Some state constitutions do require trial by jury, even though this has not always been interpreted to be applicable to the psychiatric patient. In some state constitutions, the right to trial by jury in a civil case is guaranteed to you *except* if you are accused of mental illness. In that case, you are deprived of this right.

Now, suppose you don't have very much money and you are accused of committing a crime. In most jurisdictions, you will be offered the opportunity to have an attorney represent you. What happens if you are accused of mental illness? Seventeen states provide that counsel may be supplied to someone who has none. Only five states *require* that you *get* an attorney if you request one. In the other states, you may have legal counsel only if the judge deems it appropriate.

If you don't have money, only fifteen states provide that the attorney assigned to you be compensated by the state or by the county. In other words, in some states an assigned attorney cannot be legally compensated for his actions on your behalf if you are accused of mental illness. In two states, the statutes define how much money the attorney can get when he is to be paid. In one case the maximum is $10 a day. In the other case it is $25 per day. One wonders how many attorneys look forward to receiving these cases on assignment by the court. Finally, in twelve states no legal adjudication in a courtroom need take place—nor, in fact, need a judge be involved. All that is required is a physician or psychiatrist or, in some cases, two physicians or two psychiatrists.

SO FAR, I have dealt with the problem of how you got into this institution that you didn't want to get into in the first place. What happens after you get in there? Suppose you want to get out. Suppose you want to communicate with your family. Suppose you want to communicate with your friends. Suppose you want to communicate with the judge who sent you there, or the physicians who were instrumental in getting you there. Suppose you want to communicate with the governor of the state, or with the agency in the state that operates the state hospital system. Suppose you want to communicate with anyone who would be of assistance. Again, we might look at the criminal, who does have, in most cases, the opportunity to contact his attorney throughout his incarceration. Compare him to the person who is now in the mental hospital. Eight states have statutory provisions permitting a psychiatric patient to communicate with his attorney. Only eight states. Let us assume that you are in an institution and for a variety of reasons you feel unjustifiably placed there. You wish to communicate with an outside source—such as your attorney, wife, husband, parents, or child. In most states, the superintendent of the institution is given responsibility for determining whether you may communicate with people on the outside.

Remember, you are supposed to be in there because you needed treatment. Treatment, to use a cliché, covers a multitude of sins. Treatment can be the use of mechanical restraints, chemical restraints, electroconvulsive therapy, insulin coma therapy, brain surgery—or it can be psychotherapy. It can be many things, including loss of the opportunity to communicate with the outside.

Late in the nineteenth century, word began getting out to the public of what happens to people in state and other mental hospitals. Miss Dorothea L. Dix in this country, and other reformers in many countries and many states, began investigating. Laws began to be passed by state legislators who had heard of obvious examples of mistreatment or maltreatment. However, there are only twelve states that went so far as to place in their law books any regulation on the use of mechanical restraint on a patient. Mechanical restraints may mean different things, as some of you know—cuffs, muffs, restraining jackets, and so forth.

WHILE you are in the state institution or other hospital involuntarily, what safeguards are you afforded? In no state of the United States—not a single state—does the patient have an effective right to object if the staff of the institution wants him to submit to brain surgery, electroconvulsive therapy, insulin coma therapy, or psychotherapy. In only two states is approval by a non-staff member required. In these two states, the responsible person may be the superintendent of the institution or a relative of the patient. If a husband has had his wife institutionalized (and remember that he may have initiated the action) he may be asked, "May we treat your wife in such a manner?" Of course, he will very often give his permission. He would assume, usually in all honesty on his part, that the staff of the institution is doing what is best for his wife. The evidence, however, leaves much to be desired in terms of what positive effects may be anticipated when a

human being has his brain operated upon, a procedure which has been practically abandoned, fortunately, in many states but which a few years ago was a very common practice.

Let us look at another case. The psychiatric patient believes, while in the institution or after he is discharged, that he was negligently treated while in the institution. Suppose he feels that he should not have been given electroconvulsive therapy, or should not have had his brain operated upon, or something of the kind. Suppose he comes out of one of these procedures deformed or damaged. One would imagine that in most areas of negligence he could sue the person or persons responsible. Here you meet one of the most fascinating aspects of law in the United States and a very interesting fact, though most people don't believe it.

"No psychiatric patient has ever won a case of negligence against a physician because of electroconvulsive therapy or psychosurgery despite the frequent occurrence of death and injury." The quotation comes from the American Bar Foundation, which is an agency of the American Bar Association. "No psychiatric patient has ever won a case of negligence against a physician because of electroconvulsive therapy or psychosurgery. . . ." This fact has led to vigorous dissents in cases in various courts of appeal throughout this country. A famous case occurred in the State of California, decided by the Court of Appeal of that state, some years ago. A woman had been grossly deformed as a result of electroconvulsive therapy, ending up with deformed hips, a deformed back, and almost incapable of walking. The majority, on appeal, affirmed a lower court decision that the woman could not even *enter* the case against the physicians and other staff people responsible for her condition because *she could not be a competent witness on her own behalf.*

Suppose you are in an institution, and you are stuck there for awhile, and you want to get out, and you haven't been able to communicate with others. Suppose you wanted to be re-examined by the staff of the institution to determine whether you should, in your opinion, get out. Only eleven of our states require that you be examined periodically by the institution staff. Four of the eleven do not say how often; it can be once every fifteen years, as in one court case. *No* state specifies the scope or procedure to be employed in the examination. In other words, an examination can consist of "Hello, how are you feeling?" This kind of "examination" has been accepted as being a periodic examination.

THE POINT is this: Safeguards are required. The concept "mental illness" has legal implications—some of them have already been mentioned. There are also a great number of ethical implications in terms of what human beings do to each other in a society.

There is an excellent book by a distinguished philosopher, Karl Popper, called *The Open Society and Its Enemies.* In his book, Popper argues that to have a truly open society requires that you know the consequences of your behavior when that behavior is likely to bring down the force of society upon you. Behavior and consequence should be specified—what behaviors are appropriate, what are inappropriate, what are desirable, what are undesirable, and so forth.

Rules should be specific. They should state something along the lines of our contemporary criminal law: If you are convicted of such and such a crime, you have the following obligation to society. It may be incarceration or imprisonment. It may be a fine. It may be something else or a combination of things.

The rules should be as specific as it is feasible to make them. In the adjudication of mental illness or involuntary hospitalization there is little specificity of penalty that attaches to one's behavior. In other words, you may be "a little" mentally ill but pay a tremendous penalty, or you may be "very" mentally ill but pay only small penalty. A person who is "a little" mentally ill may be in an institution the rest of his life. I say that with some basis in fact: In 1956, the last year for which we have complete figures, 36 per cent of all men admitted for the first time to a psychiatric institution died in that institution within three years; 33 per cent of all women admitted for the first time to a psychiatric institution died in that institution within three years. In the same year, 1956, 19 per cent, almost one out of every five inpatients were separated from a psychiatric institution by death. I don't say it lightly when I report that a person may be committed for life. This is what happens to a very large number of our fellow citizens.

WHAT WE often overlook, in our discussions regarding the mentally ill, is the fact that our system of laws and procedures is based on the implicit assumption that some group in our society possesses superior wisdom regarding the manner in which our lives should be lived. These are not scientifically based assumptions, nor are the basic questions involved scientific inquiries. I don't think anyone can demonstrate that he has superior wisdom on the basis of his knowledge about science. Superior wisdom does not come out of any particular professional field. I don't think we would like to see clergy-men, physicians, psychologists, attorneys, judges, or any pro-fessional group assume superior wisdom for the rest of society. Superior wisdom is not a concomitant of a person's degree from a college or university. Nor can we declare that superior wisdom comes from election to public office. We have to de-cide, each one of us, whether we are to bow to the pretensions of superior wisdom.

There is no easy answer. We can continue to accept our current procedures in regard to the psychiatric patient, or we can examine them and change them. I am not going to offer roads leading to reform or panacea. I don't have any.

I have personal points of view, though, and I am quite willing to state them. *Any* involuntary institutionalization of a person on the grounds that he is mentally ill is unacceptable —unacceptable because it assumes that we have superior wis-dom about that person's behavior, and that we know what is right and what is wrong. I don't think we "know" what is right and what is wrong. I don't think we "know" the differ-ence between good and evil in such a way that we can tell others what is good and what is evil about their behavior.

I don't think that we should tolerate a system which says, "Now that we have decided that your behavior is unacceptable, bad, or evil, you are a second-class citizen." But this is what we do today. The psychiatric patient is often very much a second-class citizen. He does not have the rights that others have, the privileges that others have, the responsibilities that others have. He has been deprived of them. The second-class citizen is a term more appropriate in regard to the psychiatric patient than to any other group it has been applied to. The American Indian, the American Negro, people of Oriental descent, and people who are members of minority religious groups have often been labeled second-class citizens. Our true second-class citizen is the psychiatric patient.

A statement of value: I do not wish to see the psychiatric patient a second-class citizen. I do not believe that he should be deprived of his civil rights or civil liberties, the prerog-atives that accompany full citizenship in this country.

I am not advocating that others should necessarily go along with this somewhat extreme point of view. I'm not saying that it is the only tenable position. I think there are many positions which can be presented quite adequately, intelligently, and with considerable wisdom. I think, however, that if we are displeased with the situation insofar as the psychiatric patient is concerned, we should undertake very intensive examinations of that which displeases us in the system and try to correct the system. For different people, different parts of this system are unpleasant or displeasing, unethical or immoral. I think that each person should examine his own conscience, his own feelings, his own beliefs, his own ethical system, and determine what it is he wants to work for. I will advocate change because I think our current system is unsatisfactory and essentially unacceptable for what Professor Popper calls the "open society," and I hope that we may have an open society in this country.

If we want to see what goes on in our system, let us not examine what professionals *say* they do as psychologists, psychiatrists, social workers, attorneys, or judges. Look at what in fact they *are* doing. I think that if you do this and are not confused by the language that is used, and if you really examine what each person does rather than what it is alleged that he does, you will find out these are quite different things. I think that what we ought to do is look at our ultra-first-class citizens—the psychiatrists, psychologists, social workers, and attorneys—and examine what they do to our second-class citizen, the psychiatric patient.

SEVEN POEMS

CARILLON CONCERT

HEARD from a boat,
  the bells fall into water,
make birds,
shape stars,
and sing
while we champagne the night.

The music floats out
like the tinkling voice
of an old woman;
the music leaps
like the tail of a horse
in the wind;
it says to someone,
to everyone,
come home.

Then its great throat
trembles into silence. . .
carillons lost forever
in the fingers of fish
feeling their way
along silver halls,
carillons dead
in the wake of white sails.

MARION SCHOEBERLEIN

Elmhurst, Illinois

TELEPHONE-CABLE CAR

A LONG THE WIRE, across the miles,
       I hear you drop the clinking coins
That pay our fare. The gripman smiles,
And to the humming cable joins
His wingèd chariot for the ride
That crawls uphill and rushes down.
By sudden shyness tongues are tied;
Time's clicking wheels we cannot drown.
With penny wisdom, counting tax,
We watch the measuring sands decline,
Anticipating at our backs
The gripman's call: "End of the line!"

On Ganges' bank, by Humber's tide,
Lovers could talk and beggars ride.

MIRIAM C. MALOY

Turlock, California

THE MORALIZER

He has three chickens
which come home to roost—
hate, envy, fear;
but in his hen-house
there are many hatches.

If I were my brother's chickens' keeper
he'd have eggs for breakfast
soup for lunch
and cold boiled carcasses for dinner.

The rest of the world could do without.

HELENE ROSENTHAL

Vancouver, British Columbia

347

CIRCLES

I HAVE deserted you have deserted me.
The dog with his tail in his mouth chews desperately.
He looks like a fool, but he knows his enemy.

What shatters love shatters all clear reflection.
We come upon odd pieces of affection,
But which came first, the defect or defection?

Then let me free and I will keep the blame.
Say I abandoned you, and curse my name
for cursing yours. All circles are the same.

ROSELLEN BROWN

Brookline, Massachusetts

RIO BO

THREE little houses
with pointed roofs,
a small green field,
a vigilant cypress tree
near a narrow stream: RIO BO
A microscopic town, true
a meaningless village, although. . .
a star always hovers above it,
a great magnificent star,
that now and then
makes eyes at the tallest branch of the cypress
of Rio Bo.
A star in love!
Who knows
if a great city has
a similar star.

ALDO PALAZZESCHI

Translated by D. M. Pettinella
New York City

HOUSESCAPE

It is not shaped of, framed in, hung on air:
but a solid space for dust.
Crumbs confabulate beneath the kitchen
chairs. Here, where I must
get up, get down; stitching and unstitching
each day's wear.

A. D. FREEMAN

Wellesley, Massachusetts

THE SOPHISTICATES

"A high class hypochondriac"
Was our hypothesis of Sal
Suffering from a malady
In her cranial cavity
That caused confusion in her face.

Swathed in lace and many presents—
All intended to improve her personality,
Which seemed somewhat extreme,—
She fled from parties to her bed
Unable to bear the pressure in her head
That came on most inconvenient days
For us who could not tolerate a deviation
From the norm
And demanded levity on all occasions.

So Sal tottered heedlessly ahead
While we denied her little game
Until the tumor caused a hemorrhage in her brain,
Forcing us to conclude with some surprise
That Sal had died.

ELAINE BARNARD

Laguna Beach, California

• DISCUSSION •

SEMANTICS AND COMMUNICATION

WILLIAM PEMBERTON*

As I see it, any specialist living in a democratic republic who has had the privilege or opportunity to collect information that is uniquely different from and potentially useful to others has the obligation to present such information so that anyone can and will understand it.

My topic is a semantic approach to communication. There are many ways of talking about semantics. The word itself comes from a Greek root that has to do with "signification." Sometimes we say that semantics is the search for the significant, the relevant, in contrast with the superficial. If someone were to ask you, "What is the most significant unsolved problem of our time?" I wonder what reply you would give? I would say man's inhumanity to man.

In a narrow sense semantics has to do with the study of meanings. In a broader and deeper sense we talk about it as the study of human evaluation, which means we study the human being as an organism which handles information. We also study the nature of the information—particularly our symbolic system (i.e., the world of words) which the organism uses to handle that information. Even more importantly, we are now beginning to study how information, once it has been internalized, determines our very reality—the ways in which we think, and feel, and behave. This information, early acquired and internalized, we call our *assumptive knowledge*.

In the past few years I have been studying the dynamics

* Clinical psychologist, Mill Valley, California.

Dr. Pemberton's last contribution to *ETC.* appeared in the September 1963 issue, Vol. XX, No. 3.

of human insult, and I find that much of human insult comes when one person questions, doubts, or criticizes the assumptive knowledge of another person. For instance, if you believe in God, and someone asks you why, or doubts the value of your belief, or is openly critical of such a belief, how do you react? Or, if someone asks you if you believe in free enterprise, in the democratic process, or more controversial issues, such as desegregation, the test ban treaty, interrupting the conceptual process by other than natural means, how quickly may you be insulted!

One of the useful bits of information about human nervous systems is that one's assumptive knowledge (which we call secondary nature) is indistinguishable from primary nature (our sensory and apperceptive processes) in determining the nature of reality.

L ET ME discuss now three different ways of talking about an experience; or, I might say, three different assumptions we can make about the nature of reality: the absolutistic, the relativistic, and the transactional. These represent roughly three stages of man's growing sophistication about the nature of himself and his cosmos. They could represent beliefs about reality that we might classify as pre-science, early science, and modern science, respectively. For purpose of demonstration, I sometimes distribute to my lecture groups bits of paper which have been dipped in phenyl-thio-carbamide, a harmless chemical which tastes bitter to approximately seventy per cent of the participants, but tasteless to the remaining thirty per cent. The papers are prepared by dipping a sheet of typing paper into the solution, drying it, and cutting it up. The result is that each person gets, comparatively speaking, the same amount of the substance. I then make a statement of fact about this event: "There is no taste in the paper," which is valid for me. Then I ask what is the thinking of the group, and get such responses as "You're wrong," "You've a different paper," "You're crazy," "Your taste buds are faulty," and the like. The accumulated scientific information: whether or not you taste the paper is determined by your inherited genes. The insult patterns started, however, are mostly because of the *assumptions* about the event; for instance, one being that if we are having the same experience we must be reacting in the same way "or else someone must be wrong" (or deficient, or what not).

Let us look again at the three different assumptions that predominate man's thinking on this kind of event—whether it is through taste, sight, hearing, or other sensory modalities.

- The assumption of the "absolutistic" person is that "the taste is in the paper" (i.e., qualities are in things).
- The assumption of the "relativistic" person is that "the taste is in me" (i.e., qualities are in me; for instance, color is determined by the cones in my eyes) ; some taste it, some do not, "so who cares?"
- The assumption of the "transactionist" is that there is a transaction going on between what's in the paper and what's going on in me. Some people react to the transaction in one way, some in another. All I can talk factually about is *my* reaction to the transaction, and then make inferences or inquire about yours.

With this assumption of modern science, based upon our knowledge about human nervous systems, I am neither defensive about my reactions nor critical of yours. We may react alike, or differently, and thus learn from one another. We can learn what we have in common, and respect each other as to the ways that we are different.

IN a similar way, we can talk about not only the similarities and differences in primary reactions, but also differences in feeling, in judgments, in standards, values, qualities, morals, meanings, which are based upon our individual and cultural collections, our secondary nature. This holds as well for our beliefs. If we find someone who has a belief or assumption about the nature of the cosmos which is different from our own, whether monotheistic, polytheistic, atheistic, pantheistic, or agnostic, the reaction is change from one of insult to one of interest, inquiry, and sharing.

An important reminder for some people is the fact that

once I understand that your reality and mine may be different (by reality meaning the way we look at things, feel about or value them, think about them) it *does not* destroy *my* reality, my values, my preferences; but it *does* make possible a respect for *your* reality. When my behavior becomes influenced by this modern assumption about the nature of reality, something in the manner of reciprocity begins to develop, simply because of the diminishing of insult, and the natural concern of homo sapiens for the survival of his own species. And please note: those who operate by the assumption of modern science re-spect the coexistence of those with other assumptions, while searching for still other assumptions more meaningful, more applicable to mankind. And while searching for these new assumptions, a self-revising process is going on.

My contention is that until we understand the assumptive level of human knowledge, until we learn something about the nature of nervous systems, and the evaluative process, the best that we can do is learn to be tolerant of others who have different assumptive knowledge. This usually means putting up with others until they learn how things "really are," and until they are "more like us," which is, of course, the right way to be. (This is, of course, a series of assertions that is based on obsolete, absolutistic assumptions.)

Once understood, and once applied, modern assumptions can clarify such diverse subjects as: morality, law, education, ethics, politics, or religion. They can increase the potential of organizational structures from the simple to the complex. They can ease relationships within the family, or within the family of nations. They can operate more effectively on the job, in the home, within, between, or among the multiple institutions of man.

A key to diminishing man's inhumanity to man (the same key to improving communication as I see it) thus lies in the direction of the dissemination of knowledge about human evaluation, how brains establish and maintain reality; how assumptive knowledge may act as a barrier to effective com-munication, whereas knowledge *about* assumptive knowledge can open the gates to deeper understanding and can increase our capacity to be human beings.

AKRESTOMIJE, ERGAHERGAHMAH, AND OHE

NELS JULEUS *

A KRESTOMIJE, ERGAHERGAHMAH, AND OHE are three languages unknown to linguists. Even those who belong to the three speech communities are not fluent in these languages, for each community consists of only the six people who developed the three languages as a project in an oral communication course at Allegheny College. The languages were constructed during three class sessions as an introduction to the study of the nature of language.[1]

"Today, we're going to construct a language," was the simple statement which introduced the unit. Three groups were quickly organized and sat staring at one another, for no one seemed to know where to begin. Indeed, many could not believe that the project was to be taken seriously.

"Agree on some sounds," the groups were directed.

"How many?" someone asked.

"It's up to you," was the answer.

One group finally decided upon ten sounds. A mathematician in the group assured his fellow students that the three and a half million possible combinations would be quite adequate for their purposes. Thus was Ergahergahmah begun. Soon, Akrestomije was brought to life with twelve sounds, and, shortly thereafter, Ohe became a language with twenty-four sounds.

For most of the students, this session was a frustrating experience. Every squeak, click, or grunt could provide their language with possible sounds. The infinite number of possibilities was quite overwhelming. On the other hand, many

* Speech and Dramatic Arts Department, Allegheny College.

[1] Akrestomije was the brainchild of Bruce Breeman, John Euliano, Karen Kemble, Bruce Leckie-Ewing, Karen Nelson, and Alan Ochsenbein. Ergahergahmah was created by Dale Andrews, Gregory Dauber, James Green, John Huse, Victor Jaccarino, and Robert Weber. Ohe was developed by Stephen Congdon, James Innis, Glen Preston, Charlene Savoca, Edward Saxman, Linda True, and Robin Williams.

felt limited by their familiarity with English. Most of the students were unable to identify the sounds of English and often confused the alphabet with the sound system. This confusion of written and oral discourse persisted throughout the unit. Few students had considered the full implications of the arbitrariness of vocal sounds which make up a language.

At the end of the class session each student was asked to make up ten words and bring them to the next class meeting.

At the second class meeting, the groups were asked to classify the words they had created. Although any feasible classification could be used, Sapir's classification of "object," "quality," and "action" seemed practical.

The important principle developed at this meeting was that words do not have a necessary connection with their referents. The relationship between a given sound or group of sounds and the thing to which it refers is arbitrary. In Akrestomije, an "ima" might just as well have been called a "jat." In Ohe, a "ha" might have been called "da." And, in Ergahergahmah, what is called a "booingemm" might just as easily have been classed as an "ergahbooingemm." This concept, so easily escaped from when referring to English words, is dramatically demonstrated with a "do-it-yourself" language.

For further development during this class meeting, each group was asked to consider what use might be made of "inflection," "function words," and "sentence structure." One student expressed difficulty in understanding that the rules he was making up for word relationships were the grammar of his language. A number of students were beginning to disagree about pronunciation of sounds in new words. The three groups soon discovered that when they wanted a particular convention for their language, the majority ruled. They soon understood, too, that if the speech community were to extend its influence beyond the limits of the group, persuasion or domination would be the means to that end. Further, the differences between each person's pronunciation and opinions of what should stand for what provided an apt illustration of how dialects develop.

Homework consisted of more vocabulary building.

THE third day of language construction consisted of putting the final touches on the language. Students were asked to consider whether their language would have articles, singular and plural, words for days of the week or months, verb-noun-adjective endings, numbers, words for yes and no, and words for greetings and farewell. The questions about these possibilities were suggestions and not prescriptions, for the intent of the third day was to demonstrate to the students how language affects our perception of reality and to show how our language conditions our view of another culture.

One girl observed that she had never felt so "stupid" before. She expressed the difficulty she had in "thinking" about, and in, the language she was working on. She felt limited by the language she helped to create. Most students complained of this feeling of frustration. The complete arbitrariness of the language was disturbing. They felt limited in their ability to communicate in this new language. All reacted to the restraint on their "creativity" provided by their knowledge of English.

That language conditions perception is particularly clear in the case of Ergahergahmah. The students in this group had early decided to restrict the vocabulary of their language to words for things in the room in which they worked. This view of the world was their limited frame of reference. Thus, for example, they translated "our Father who art in heaven" as "teacher in ceiling." With no form of the verb "to be" there was little danger of confusion resulting from the "is" of identity. In Akrestomije, opposition is shown by reversing words. Sky is "jo" and ground is "oj," good is "kaj" and bad is "jak," and love is "oam" while hate is "mao." This bi-polarization of terms, so common in English, has carried over a two-valued orientation into this language with a vengeance. Ohe, which means "happy," so named because this group needed to feel optimistic about the project, like the other languages is regular; similar to Esperanto, verbs are formed by adding "o", nouns by adding "a", modifiers by adding "e". There are no conjunctions, no articles, and no pronouns in this language. Opposite relationships are indicated by prefixing "u", thus, "ba" is man while "uba" is woman. It is clear from this convention, despite the fact that there were three women in the group, that this community gives a superior place to its men.

The afternoon of the third day, representatives of each group met, typed up the rules and vocabularies of their languages, and dittoed them for distribution to the entire class. The fourth and final day of this unit was spent in discussing the ways a particular language conditions an individual's perception of reality and the forces of change within a speech community.

Students were asked to write a paper telling what they had derived from the assignment. Generally, reactions were favorable. Some found the problem far more difficult than they had originally supposed. Some noted that they had never thought much about language, and this kind of assignment proved to be an eye opener. Some commented that language study seemed more exciting than they had imagined.

This much is clear, however, one of the ways to find out how little we know about language is to try to construct a new one.

GESTURES AS EXPRESSION IN THE MIDDLE EAST

HAIG KHATCHADOURIAN*

PROFESSOR LEO HAMALIAN'S sketch, "Communication by Gesture in the Middle East," in the March 1965 *ETC.*, is an interesting preliminary venture into an intriguing aspect of Middle Eastern life and culture. It would add to our much-needed understanding of this area for psychologists, sociologists, and semanticists to make a detailed study of gestures as communication, and—something which Professor Hamalian does very briefly—*relate it to the various aspects of the culture.* In this way, the precise role which gestures play in communication in the broadest sense, and the reasons for the extensive use of gestures in the area, will be revealed.

For example, an attempt should be made to discover to what extent gestures are used (1) to *reinforce* or *dramatize* verbal communication, and (2) as a *substitute* for verbal communication: for conveying what people would not, or dare not, normally attempt to convey verbally. (The "sexual" gestures Professor Hamalian mentions are one kind of illustration of this.) In general, it would be instructive to discover whether, or to what extent, gestures serve to compensate for the overt "make-believe" so prevalent in this culture: the hiatus between what one says and does on the one hand, and what one privately feels and thinks on the other hand.

Concerning the actual contents of the essay, my experience as a native of the area confirms a good deal of what Professor Hamalian says about the "meaning" of the various gestures mentioned. However, his interpretation of some of the gestures is, to my mind, rather oversimplified. Similarly oversimplified, or only partly true, are some of the generalizations (always dangerous in this , as in other aspects, of social life) which he makes. Examples of the former are:

"Gestures in the Arab world are apparently confined to the hands. . . ." (p. 44) We should certainly add: and the arms,

---

* American University, Beirut, Lebanon.

SEPTEMBER 1966   DISCUSSION

and to a lesser extent, the legs and other parts of the body. And this is not confined to "experts."[1]

"Gestures appear to be associated with the expression of three main emotions. . . ." (p. 44) We should add: uncertainty, puzzlement, surprise, and other psychological states, experiences, or feelings.

"Gesture is associated with the level of education. . . ." (p. 44) Yes, but it is also a matter of individual temperament, and perhaps also, of social milieu.

"The gestures are usually sex-linked. . . ." (p. 44) This is true of some gestures; but quite a number of gestures are common to both sexes. As for ". . . women seem to depend upon gesture far less than men do," this is hard to substantiate in the absense of proper empirical studies. Similiarly with "Men use the gesture also [lifting the chin upwards to indicate the negative] but without the ability to bestow it with the range of meanings that women do."[2] (p. 46)

As for Professor Hamalian's interpretation of specific gestures, I find some of them quite dubious or puzzling, or only partly true. Thus (pp. 44-45), his remarks about the dance apply, at best, to the belly dance and other dances performed in such places as nightclubs. They certainly do not apply, say, to the Lebanese *Debké*, and various Palestinian, and other folk dances. (Love is one of the common themes of folk dances; but this is quite a different matter from what Professor Hamalian says.) Again, I am puzzled by the statement that "In Syria and Lebanon, these meanings" [i.e., the meaning of the locking of the little fingers and the locking of the second

---

[1] Facial expressions, which are not, of course, gestures, are also important as a means of communication between people in this culture —as it is in other cultures as well.

[2] Shaking the head is also a common gesture used to indicate the negative; while nodding is a common gesture used to indicate the affirmative. This illustrates the rather important point that *different* gestures, as in the case of words and sentences, may "mean" the same thing. A little later (e.g. in the case of winking) we shall also see how *one and the same* gesture may be used in different contexts to "mean" different things.

fingers] seem to be reversed." (p. 47) I have not noticed any such difference in Lebanon at least, during my long stay here. The statement on page 48, beginning "When one feels happiness or joy . . ." is true. But the gesture mentioned, I have always observed, is performed in the presence of the enemy or enemies, etc. in question, never in his or their absence. The words meaning, literally, to "crack and die"—of envy, are frequently repeated while the gesture is performed.

Finally, I do not find some of the things Hamalian says on pp. 48-49 about "sexual" gestures, confirmed in my experience. Running the hand over the hair, and twisting or running the hand over the mustache, are, I think, still fairly common reactions to the proximity of young ladies—especially among the uneducated. But unlike winking, they frequently do not, it seems to me, have any definite "meaning." The former, at least, are probably often semi-unconscious and automatic—a half-spontaneous and hurried attempt to look attractive or presentable. But even winking is rarely as strong and explicit as "I would [now] like to sleep with you. . . ." Also, it is often used playfully among friends of both sexes, to indicate some adolescent "intrigue" or "secret understanding," or to signal to those one wishes to take into one's confidence that the particular person—or one of his friends—is about to play a prank on some unsuspecting victim in the company. A scrub-brush motion of the fingers is also often no more than an intimation of friendship between people, even in the case of persons of the opposite sex. The other "sexual" gestures mentioned on page 49, I have not observed at all. They may be used in Syria, among some Moslems, where probably Professor Hamalian (I assume) observed them.

IT would be well to observe, finally, that there are at least two "kinds" of gestures in this part of the world, as probably everywhere else to some extent: first, more or less conventional and stylized gestures, usually consciously performed, which possess some more or less precise "meaning" or set of "meanings" (those Professor Hamalian discusses are all of this kind); and secondly, more or less unconscious, non-voluntary gestures that possess no specific "meaning," convey no ideas or thoughts, but which reinforce or dramatize and intensify what is being verbally conveyed. These may be labelled "emotive and dynamic gestures." In every case, they spontaneously evince the speaker's feelings, emotions or attitudes. There is a good deal of both kinds of gesture in this culture, though I notice that both are becoming less prevalent with the younger generations, partly at least, with the spread of education (cf., Hamalian, p. 44) and increased westernization.

OF GROOVIES AND FANCY WORDS

MAURICE A. CRANE *

ON MARCH 16, 1965, Lord Conesford arose in the House of Lords and asked if Her Majesty's Director of Public Prosecutions had considered the criminal implications of a paragraph which appeared on the sleeve of a record made by the pop singing group, the Rolling Stones. He proceeded to quote:

> Cast deep into your pockets for loot to buy this disc of groovies and fancy words. If you don't have bread, see that blind man, knock him on the head, steal his wallet, and lo and behold, you have the loot. If you put in the boot, good. Another one sold.

The Parliamentary Under-Secretary to the Home Office, Lord Stonham, although holding no brief for the paragraph as literature, offered his official opinion that the words did not in themselves constitute a criminal offense.

Abashed, Lord Conesford asked, "Do I understand that inciting people to assault, rob, and kick the blind is beyond the reach of criminal law? If that is so, is there anything the Government proposes to do?"

The Under-Secretary replied: "We all agree that these words are offensive to a degree although they are not regarded as incitement to criminal offense. If it is any consolation, the researches I made during the weekend show that even where the words are intelligible in a 'pop' song they are not regarded as important, *and the devotees pay even less attention to the blurb on the envelope.*"

Lord Stonham's abrupt shift of attention from the ornamental to the communicative uses of language qualifies him for sponsoring the most ambitious leap attempted by a *non sequitur* in the current Parliamentary session. He is absolutely correct about the amount of meaningful content in the current crop of British pop tunes. At their most articulate they declare

---

* Associate Professor of Humanities, Michigan State University, East Lansing, Michigan.

nothing more specific than "There she was just a-walkin'
down the street, singin' doo wah ditty ditty, doo wah ditty
ditty." Pop lyricists work within rigidly strict limitations.
Their words must conform to the rhythmic pattern of three
electric guitars and a drum, and they must not do anything to
detract from the "sound"—that is, the essential twang of the
background.

U P UNTIL modern times, the words of popular songs
have been valued most highly if they told a story as well
as blending with the melody and mood. But what was required of ballads and show tunes does not hold for the Mods
and Rockers. The assignment of meaning to the words they
use would diminish the value of the lyrics. The song as a
whole is a kind of humorous comment on the meaninglessness
of the world both singer and listener find themselves in. The
British teenager's mind is not so literal and gullible that it
can be duped into taking pop lyrics for serious statements.

Not so with the blurb. Its chief purpose is to convince
the casual reader to purchase the album in his hands. The blurb
writer directs his communication at a reader whom he wishes
to entice into a specific type of action. The writer who offended
the sensibilities of the House of Lords and many others in
Britain was attempting to convey to the reader a shared "hip-
ness" by (1) using the ghoul humor currently "in" with the
under-twenties and by (2) seeming to fall into the rhythm-
and-rhyme pattern which the naturally "beat" employ in normal speech.

There is more than coincidental rhyme in the lilting movement from *bread* to *head* to *behold* to *loot* to *boot* to *sold*.
Both *bread* and *loot* are "in" terms for money, and the suggestions about the *head* and the *boot* seem to be dictated more
by the need for facile rhyme than by anything else. Americans
remember the fuss made by clergymen in the early fifties when
strumming Tennesseeans were suggesting that the dancer
"Rock and roll to glorify . . . [his] soul." The same phenomenon was at work: the need for rhyme coupled with a limited
vocabulary.

The apparent greed of the blurb writer and the heinous crime he proposes are both so outlandishly overdrawn as to preclude the possibility of their being taken as seriously as, say, the milder suggestion that the reader find his pennies lying on a newsstand or in a collection plate. If there is any crime here, it is literary rather than legal. The devices intended to produce laughter produced anger instead.

COMEDY frequently grows out of the unexpected, but we like to control our shock by allowing the unexpected complete freedom only within expected limits. When we buy tickets for a musical fantasy we expect the "8:30" on our tickets to refer to an 8:30 we understand and the numbers on the tickets to match numbers on corresponding seats, no mat-

ter how we suspend disbelief in order to accept the onstage situation.

We do not read a contemporary preface to a new edition of *The Iliad* or *Coriolanus* or Carlyle's *French Revolution* with the same tolerance we exercise on the prose that follows. Prefaces, like blurbs, are read for what they propose rather than for what they are. When we read both Lucretius and Thomas Aquinas on God, or the Order of the Universe, we know that at least one of them is propositionally mistaken, but we read both with equal pleasure. If an editor were to write introductions to both, agreeing with the *position* of each, we would have to brand him a hypocrite. For an advertisement or an introduction or a criticism, even at its most frivolous, is expected to tell "truths" that the reader can verify.

The record-jacket blurb that prompted Lord Conesford to rise in the House of Lords says, for instance, if you are the type of person who finds my rhyming language and ghoulish humor attractive you will certainly like the kind of thing the Rolling Stones produce on this record well enough to want to buy a copy of your own. The only difference between this appeal and an appeal to join in the purchasing of an "in" brand of cigarettes or neckties or liquor is that one can buy these commodities only for what they "are," since they don't "say" anything in the way a commodity made out of words does. Even so, most people in the arts defended *Lolita* for what it was as opposed to what it said.

This may prove the old maxim about not telling a book by its cover. For if the dustjacket blurb for *Lolita* proposed not only that one buy the book but that he join an organization dedicated to furthering the philosophy and actions of the fictional Humbert Humbert as well, we might have seen the matter come before the U.S. Senate. It would have had to be an extremely funny and transparently satirical blurb to escape the condemnation of some legislators, apparently even more transparent than the ad for the Rolling Stones' latest collection of groovies and fancy words.

Perhaps a scare like that would send the dustjacket writers out of the fiction business altogether.

INTERNATIONAL RELATIONS:
ELEMENTARY LEVEL

FLORENCE YEO STOCKING*

"WE ARE holding hands," they wrote. "Our two schools are sister schools—one in America, one in Japan. Growing in understanding and friendship we will go holding hands with each other, so please remember us."

We are listening to a tape recording which the Shokuryu School in Kyoto has recently sent us. Fifth- and sixth-grade pupils sing twelve songs, one for each month of the year. In a radio contest the chorus was chosen to perform with the University of Kyoto's Mandolin Orchestra. For the first time since World War II, this orchestra had resumed its thirty-eight-year custom of playing host to, and accompanying, an elementary group in a year-end concert.

The young voices sing out in strength. They enunciate the Japanese words precisely, and it helps us to understand. But it is the enchanting melodies that carry their message in full. At the conclusion of the formal part of the recorded program, there are five *a cappella* songs of the type traditionally sung by youngsters while playing such games as *Hane tsuki* (battledore and shuttlecock—a kind of badminton), and *Se Se Se* (patty cake—a hand-clapping game in which the speed increases until the two players giggle, and miss, and howl at their own clumsiness). In these unaccompanied songs, the voices are clear and close. And we are listening.

We are looking, too, at watercolor scenes of their daily activities, which are for us an intimate diary: a sleeping boy on *futon* with catcher's mitt nearby; a crowd of picnicking children, with lunch boxes and chopsticks; ten bathers at the public bath; a scene in a bowling alley. Hanako has sketched herself in traditional kimono. "When wearing Japanese kimono," she writes in English, "I seem to be gentle."

* Colonial Acres Elementary School, San Lorenzo, California. Mrs. Stocking's last contribution to *ETC.*, "The Not-Word Was the Thing," appeared in the December 1963 issue.

These gifts are the most recent exchange between our schools. Earlier this year, for a PTA meeting, our class had arranged an exhibit of thirty children's paintings which had been a bon voyage gift to me, the teacher, when I visited the Kyoto school. A news photographer attended our exhibit, at which kimono-clad pupils acted as guides. "Wonderful," he said, and he snapped the display of Japanese Art and the costumed children as well.

The newspaper photograph was sent to our friends in Japan, and a reporter *there* saw it and said, "This is indeed wonderful!" And he, in turn, snapped the Kyoto pupils looking at a picture of their paintings on exhibit in America. Makoto Hase wrote from Kyoto that he was "surprised that girls in United States wore the kimono," and that he had jumped for joy when he saw the photograph of his painting on display. "I felt that I was like a famous artist," he said. "I think it is good to be holding hands and exchanging friendships together."

Teacher Soga wrote: "I have no doubt that the bonds of friendship between our two schools can become part of the United States–Japanese relations." Small elementary schools playing a part in international relations? It is already happening.

WIDESPREAD RIPPLES, small waves lapping at a far shore. What of the first pebble; how and why was it tossed? The beginning was small indeed. One word; not even a word, really, just an utterance. A small, ugly sound—in rejection— more than a year before.

"Ughf!" our Nancy had said.

It was noontime, early in the school year. We were waiting for the bell to signal the time for lunch. The teacher's tour of Japan had only recently ended. Her thoughts strayed. She remembered lacquered trays bearing bowls of fragrant soup, and seafood in tangy sauce, and she made off-hand mention of a food she had especially enjoyed in Tokyo. It was then that Nancy had spoken up quickly: "Ughf! In Japan they eat all their food *raw*!"

After the noon recess, we decided to skip the social studies lesson and just sit around and talk for a while. Eleven-year-olds being as they are, they returned quickly and volubly to the subject of food. All, that is, except our three Nisei pupils. They were tense and still.

Linda was first. "If Nancy's right, the food they eat in Japan must be—well, just awful!"

"Yeah," said Sam. "I wouldn't want to eat *my* food raw."

Other comments came tumbling out as the voicing of one private assumption invited a host of others:

- Fish is eaten raw. They just catch a fish—and eat it!
- Seaweed is scooped up, a tangled mess from the sea, and eaten.
- Rice is *all* they ever eat.
- For vegetables they have to dig roots out of the ground.
- Nobody drinks anything but tea.
- Coffee is unknown. I don't know about milk.
- There are no cookies or cakes.

They summed it up thus: In Japan, food is in short supply. It is poorly prepared, nutritionally inadequate, and altogether revolting. Tom said that *we* couldn't live on it. Later, when they learned what the Japanese eat, and how they prepare and serve their food, twelve pupils thought "those exotic meals" a major reason for someday traveling to Japan. And Skip suggested that our cafeteria should serve sukiyaki once a week.

THE ASSUMPTIONS branched out into other areas, and, aided by competitively vivid imaginations, the list grew. Many pupils agreed that "real" poverty is the general rule in Japan. "Everybody's poorer than a church mouse," Tom volunteered. "My dad said so. He used to be in the Navy." It was a great surprise, later, to discover that our own TV, radio, and newspapers were reporting that Japan had a high degree of industrial growth and economic prosperity. "We *could* have known about it all along," Nancy said as she smiled furtively at Muriko. But in the beginning we had thought:

- All the people have a poor, hard life.
- Boys work long hours with no time for play or study.
- The men are strong and practice "killer" sports, like jujitsu.
- Team sports are probably not played.
- Japanese girls don't play games at all because those tight kimonos would interfere.
- They must work all day long in the rice fields.
- They must grow long hair—probably long enough to sit on.
- The women must walk behind their husbands on the street.

Further, our list revealed, we thought:
- Families must live in poor, unpainted houses with no window glass—only paper.
- They have no furniture, probably no radio or TV (17 of the 33 children have Japanese transistor radios at home).
- They manufacture only cheap things for dime stores (the children were familiar with Japanese cameras, binoculars, silks, and pearls).
- Probably there are few autos and taxis.
- Schools are rare; education is neglected.
- The spoken language doesn't even *sound* like a language.
- The written word—"well, it looks like a lot of hentracks and make no sense."

A ND THERE WAS the matter of the Japanese *bath*. The subject was frequently hinted at, but no specific assumptions were voiced about it. Eyes darted in interest, then lowered in embarrassment. "What is it really like?" a brave one asked. When they learned that people wash and shower first, then soak in deep, hot pools—often families and friends relaxing and visiting together—they thought it frankly sensible. And they agreed that when they travel to Japan they will first have a bath and take time to enjoy the deep, hot soaking. It sounded like much more fun than their own bothersome jumpin-and-out baths at home. ("After you *do* get into the tub somebody always yells at you to hurry.")

Here within the walls of our classroom, a tide was rising. Here, a gathering sea of beliefs and convictions and startling ideas. We were buffeted by the waves of disagreement between those who had *heard* and those who *knew*. Our confusion mounted until we were overwhelmed—swamped in a sea of our own making. And from our small, turbulent sea, one widespreading ripple reached beyond our classroom and lapped at a distant shore.

MURIKO WEPT. "It's not *like* that—it just isn't!" she wailed. Then all was still.

"I wonder," said Dan after a moment, "what folks in Japan are thinking about us."

The need for research about the people in Japan was clear. A check on our confused notions was in order. We observed ourselves—in action—repeating hearsay or a guess as if it were a truth; we discovered, perhaps for the first time, that we talked simply to be talking; we saw how easy it was to agree with Doug (who was popular) and to disagree with Gary (who wasn't). We heard ourselves answer questions which were silly or unanswerable or both.

What questions *could* we ask for which we could find answers? Certain questions were already in mind. The awareness that our assumptions needed exploring got us off to a good start. And in this way, thirty-three pupils began what has grown into an international project. Among other things, we:

- Talked to people who had lived in Japan.
- Looked at documentary, travel, and art films.
- Scoured libraries, museums, Japanese markets.
- Brought in objects of Japanese origin.
- Watched newspapers, TV, magazines for news reports.

Shig's mother, a former instructor in Kyoto, was our number-one resource person. It was she who had arranged the teacher's visit to the Japanese school in the first place. Now she did all the work of translating from Japanese into English and vice versa, and she helped us in countless other ways. Our debt to her was enormous. The balance was somewhat restored as her shaky English steadily improved under the pressure of pupils' questions. More than once, when she faltered in an explanation as she groped for words, a pupil urged: "Go ahead, Mrs. Shigekawa. Just say it in your own way." And the words came.

Muriko's mother visited us. She wore kimono, obi, zori. Her hobby was making historical dolls, and from her rich collection we learned not only about traditional costumes but also about much of Japan's history.

Al's father came one day. He discussed pictographs and the development of calligraphy. He demonstrated writing with the brush and taught us to form the numbers from one to ten. And he gave us a language lesson, and taught us to say *konnichiwa,* and *arigato,* and more. In response to class request, Al continued till year's end with daily five-minute language lessons. In this painless way we acquired a vocabulary of nearly two hundred Japanese words.

Volunteers presented special reports to the class, mainly about the assumptions which had been our point of departure. Display charts and demonstrations were prepared, skits were performed, food and chopsticks were brought in. We did brush painting, we were shown jujitsu holds, we watched a parasol dance. We spoke in Japanese, heard stories, sang songs, and tasted seaweed, rice candy, and osushi—with eel. And we listened to reports—reports about food, customs, education, trade, art, politics, and more. All the while, we were *consciously* checking our findings against our original assumptions. And many of those assumptions burst like soap bubbles without leaving a trace. Some ideas were not changed, of course. Jim said that the seaweed actually tasted *worse* than he had expected it to.

Our investigation continued. Sue remarked one day: "This is like a laboratory with scientists—testing *this* and checking *that,* and not always looking in books for the information, either." And we felt quite mature to be *aware* of using scien-

371

tific method to test our own beliefs and ideas. *Idea—experiment—report—revise*, the texts said. Here was a demonstration of that method in our own everyday affairs.

Our activities were reported to the student council, and representatives came to have a look. An idea took shape. Our school would undertake an "album project." Snapshots and articles would be gathered from each class, assembled in an album, and sent to the Japanese school to show its pupils "something about life in the United States and how we do thing here at school." It must be a beautiful, bilingual album which would say *arigato gozaimasu* for the gift of paintings we had already received. Committees were formed to plan and make the album, and our principal photographed us at work and at play during the next few weeks.

We were well pleased with the album that went to Sho-kuryu Shogakko last year—pleased to be reaching out in a hands-across-the-sea gesture, and delighted to be finding new friends. But there was more. Thorough evaluation of the project revealed that these experiences had helped us greatly:

• *To learn* in reliable ways about the people of Japan, and to abandon many false assumptions about them.

• *To recognize* the probability that we harbor false ideas about people and situations—perhaps even about those that are *closer home*.

• *To discover* that the scientific method of investigation can be used in daily affairs, and that being *aware* of using the method is part of the method.

• *To realize* that by helping us to understand others, this kind of investigation leads us to understand ourselves better.

• *To understand* that in learning to live in a constantly changing world, we can be guided in planning for the future —and guided, as well, toward saner and happier living now.

TESTING GENERAL SEMANTICS THROUGH A DISCIPLINE

BARBARA G. COLLINS*

THIS PAST SPRING I took an archaeology field course at the University of California, Los Angeles, in an effort to personally engage in, observe, and retrace the steps by which a person in a tightly controlled discipline advances from concrete experiences to abstract observations. My experience did, and still does (I have now become a lab helper to an archaeologist), support my reason for taking this course, as well as providing me with some new reasons.

I also wanted to test at first-hand—instead of second or third-hand, as has mostly been my experience—the validity of some of the precepts of general semantics. I hoped this would serve to remind me that general semantics, like other disciplines, took its course from concrete observations, before becoming organized into a system of its own. I felt that for myself, I had done too much talking about talking with other people; that our talking had gotten too far from the concrete experiences which had provided the initial basis for our abstractions; that our examples had become outworn; and that the experiences we cited to back up our statements had been too discontinuous in duration or observation to serve as evidence or to provide more than an impetus to the much-needed research necessary for our drawing any kind of conclusions.

Many general semanticists are fond of saying that we "do too much talking," as if talking in itself helped to destroy the event in our consciousness. I would contend that this conclusion need not follow. Instead, I would suggest that our failure is that we often forget that all talking is *about* something and that, in order to be continually in touch with the subject external to us, we must continue to talk about it as much as we can. Furthermore, we must explore the many different ways we can talk about our subject. To talk as much as we can keeps us conscious of our subject, rather than going to

* Lab helper, Archaeological Survey, University of California, Los Angeles.

sleep amid a welter of non-verbal experiences which soon lose their shape and immediacy because of our taboo of not talking about them.

One of the most impressive things to first hit the beginning archaeologist is the abundance of stone artifactual material, and accordingly, he tries to fit it into some existing pattern of experience. Usually, though, about all the beginner knows about stone artifacts is arrowheads; and he learns immediately that all stone artifacts are *not* arrowheads. "Well, then," the beginner asks, "what are all these amorphous-looking blobs?" A very natural question, for the world the student knows takes very different shapes from an older one. The surfaces are different, the tools are often mutliple instead of single in use, and the functional emphasis of all the parts in one tool is different. For instance, in one stone tool, in contrast to a modern one, the tool is often worked in only a limited area, the purpose of the tool-maker being to stress the immediately functional part—such as the edge of a piece of stone—and to merely require that the not-immediately functional part be physically manageable. The lines of the stone tool do not usually excel in being excessively geometrical, curvilinear, nor balanced in composition. In the beginning, the student often mistakes a flake, which is the wastage of a tool-in-the-making, for the tool itself, as often the untouched flake takes a fracture and pattern that resembles the geometrical and curvilinear lines of the world the student knows. The type of surfaces exhibited by the stone tool are often deceptive, as smooth surfaces lead the student into thinking that the piece of stone must be a finished product, as most of the modern items in the beginner's experience are smoothly finished. In reality, though, smooth surfaces in this case are often either due to the nature of the material, such as obsidian, or else haven't been worked extensively to become rough with use or extensive shaping. In addition, the student is so accustomed to specialized tools of a certain type that he is neither aware that one tool can serve several purposes—as a hammerstone can also become a serviceable pestle—nor has he had the opportunity to enlarge his definition of specialization enough to realize that because a tool is multiple by *his*

definition that it does not thereby lose its ability to be specialized at the same time.

A NOTHER PROBLEM to occupy the beginning student in
archaeology, which is one of particular interest to general semanticists, is that of terminology: what do you *call* this
piece of stone? The question is complex. First, the student
wants a set of established terms so that when he talks about
an artifact, everybody will know what kind of a thing he is
talking about. There is some agreement about terms among
professionals, or else the professionals have learned several
terms, instead of one term, for a given object. However, each
professional tends to have his own set of classificatory names
which he feels to be more accurate than anyone else's. Consequently, if a student appeals to several professionals, he may
get several terms for the same item, instead of one, which
makes him wonder whether he will be understood by all professionals and if, indeed, the multiplicity of terms designates
one, or several types, of things. In addition, sometimes the
beginning student will ask what to call something, hoping
that the name to be given the object will either describe a like
item in his own experience or how this item was used. Both
sides of the question, "What do you *call* it?," however, illus-
trate a very important, though simple fact: that time depth
and the absence of these ancient tool-makers cannot be fully
realized through the present, and that names for the artifacts
and the uses they were put to represent, in the world of the
present, a somewhat organized set of guesses and a declaration
to continue research.

Related to the problem of terminology are the problems
the beginning student faces when he has to fill out the section
labeled "object" on the record sheet. First, perhaps, I should
pay tribute to the archaeology record sheet by explaining its
multiplicity of functions. It covers: who was responsible for
the artifacts and at what time; how to find it again (spatial
dimension—in the museum'; geographic location; depth
(often, but not always, the time dimension); material (physical composition—but also often suggesting availability, functional ability, value hierarchy, and geographic location);

object (tool type—mostly personal observation) ; and remarks (ranging from "observations" to hypotheses). Often, the beginning student can fairly easily fill in every heading but that of "object." Quite naturally, categories other than "object" are easier to fill in, as these other categories are on a measurable and therefore different order of abstraction from "object," which is hypothetical. All the other categories provide a time/space environment for the artifact, and the beginning student comes to appreciate this. Still, what should the student do about filling in the very limited space labeled "object," a command to make an abstraction? One way to fill in this space is personally to examine, carefully, the whole lot. You can examine it a number of ways: its outline (whether it is triangular, diamond-shaped, ovate, rectangular, etc.) ; its length-width-thickness ratio; its seeming use; what kind of motions would produce such-and-such an effect; its degree of workedness, etc. All these ways of examination are personal. You can also fill in the "object" category by what you think the more professional person's classification would be (not an easy problem, as much of that person's definitions are given ones, and are therefore unverbalized, except to himself). Or you can learn to fill in the category "object" by watching the more professional person sort the assemblage over a period of time, and discover that he may change his opinion from day-to-day about what to call the different items in his collection.

I have named only a very few of the problems the beginning archaeologist copes with when he tries to deal with California lithic material in the light of his previous experience. I have also touched on only a few aspects in a semester of Southern California archaeology of concern to the general semanticist. Still, I hope that my experience and my brief observations on my experience are compelling enough to encourage some general semanticists to put general semantics to the test through a discipline such as archaeology.

• BOOK REVIEWS •

Criticism of Education

How Children Fail, by John Holt. New York: Pitman Publishing Corporation, 1964. 181 pp. $4.50

The Tyranny of Schooling, by Lewis Anthony Dexter. New York: Basic Books, Inc., 1964. 176 pp. $4.50

ALTHOUGH both writers take issue with current educative practices, their objectives are quite different. Holt would like to see methods developed that would extend education. Dexter proposes that education be limited to the academically select.

John Holt while teaching at elementary and junior high levels in several private schools, wrote and collected anecdotal memos about his classroom experiences and what these engendered in him. From them the author has selected a number of entries dated from 1958 to 1961 and grouped them into four sections and a summary:

• *Strategy.* This refers to strategems that children use to outflank and to get the best of the teacher. A basic assumption seems to be that children feel they are in school to outsmart the teacher rather than to learn.

• *Fear and Failure.* The author's feeling that children with fears are more failure-prone coincides with a mainstream of thinking among educators.

• *Real Learning.* When the learner can select what he is going to learn, real learning may take place. Then the learning may be lasting, relevant, useful, and utilized rather than be superimposed tasks that must be completed with little meaning and much harm.

• *How Schools Fail.* Holt's position seems to be that schools are too much like machines that attempt to mold children to adult specifications. In the process, joy of living and interest in reality devolve towards stupidity.

How Children Fail is more of an autobiography than it is a study of children. The author writes, "This past year I had some terrible students. I failed more kids, mostly in French and Algebra, than did all of the teachers in the school together." (Perhaps another title could have been "How I Fail Children.")

There seems to have been a need by Holt to verbalize internal pressures that arose from daily classroom impacts. Possibly, verbal catharsis may have helped diminish an apprehension about how children manipulate teachers. The memoranda about children's strategy against learning and against teachers extend only to 1959; the other sections of the book include notations into 1961.

REPEATEDLY, I felt that imputation of children's motives was being handled like analytical observation; that judgments were being launched from inferences that were needlessly brittle for lack of "to me" shock absorbers; and that much speculation was based on assumptions that came to be treated as facts. In one of his longest anecdotes (pp. 50-56), the author sees a child ("about forty feet away") at a concert, decides she is seriously retarded, primarily by a "sick downturning of the mouth," and discusses the child in particular, and retardation in general, without ever having spoken a word with the girl or with her "very attractive, suburban-looking mother."

Even his more descriptive presentations frequently are marred by oversimplifications and overstatements:

> Foundations . . . seem ready at the drop of a hat to spend millions of dollars on grandiose projects which produce, in the main, only publicity and doctoral dissertations. . . . It's their way of solving the knotty problem of understanding; just say there is no such thing. Apparently this view is currently in fashion among psychologists. . . .

Teach them to say everything that Einstein knew, and hey, presto! another Einstein!

It's amazing what nonsense people will believe.

Of course, this notion fits neatly into behaviorism, which is still very much in fashion, despite all it cannot explain.

His summary reflects changes in Holt's perspectives as well as some summation. Earlier Holt had written in various sections:

All children need to succeed; but . . . success should not be quick or easy, and should not come all the time.

A good batting average in baseball is .300; a good batting average in life is a great deal lower than that. . . .

The unbelievable incompetence of some of the kids sometimes drives me wild. They can't find anything. They have no paper or pencil when it's time for work. Their desks are a mess. They lose library books. (Following a class success experience with fractions) I am almost afraid to try it again. Some of them might be able to do this without the rods; most of them, not.

But in the summary, Holt says we must not coerce children because that makes them afraid and prone to failure. "School should be a great smörgasbord of intellectual, artistic, creative, and athletic activities," from which each child can take as he wants.

Amid much of this book's intensional chaff there are some grains worth milling. And in spite of the strident outcries of frustrated "allnesses," there sounds a note of concern about children as well as people in general.

Lewis Anthony Dexter, in his book, assumes wide-spread and immutable stupidity that necessitates keeping people at arm's length. His polemic argues and implies that compulsory schooling imposes harmful and unnecessary burdens on the retarded students and even creates some of their major handicaps and problems; that the stupid, even more than ethnic minorities, are discriminated against because they are denied the right of democratic choice as to whether or not they prefer to remain stupid; that high grade retardates, if they were free of school-promoted stigma, could readily be absorbed into the general population and remain unrecognizable within it; and that child labor laws can be too much of a good thing, because they bar the retardates for too long a time from a useful place in the labor market.

Dexter proposes that schooling is different from education. He feels that schools do teach children to observe schedules and to practice reasonable punctuality, cleanliness, neatness, and other conformable habits, because these are not so painful as academic schooling. He urges that it is more important to teach children to "swing back to virtue" than to teach them to get ahead through intellectual skills. Nowhere does the author examine what handicaps and problems would be super-imposed by conformancy-centered curricula.

After freely generalizing about the inadequacies of com-pulsory schools and egalitarian values (one chapter is titled "A Democratic Dilemma: Compulsory Equality or the Liberty to Be Stupid?"), Dexter indicates that practical proposals cannot be generalized because answers must be placed within a spe-cific administrative and social context. However, he does pro-pose as a solution to the pangs of stupidity that most state-supported junior and community colleges be shut down; that all government aids to mediocre college students be withdrawn; that the same money be invested in better ways; and that we return to the university which serves only the professionally-aimed and the intellectually hungry as long as the professions and motivations can be considered genuine.

A MONG his closing thoughts, Dexter raises a question about benevolent protection for retardates: "Or would it not be better to try to organize something for retardates like the Gheel community for psychotics?" (Happily, there is no men-tion of sterilization.)

Dexter encourages that judgments be made from personal opinions in preference to reasoning from scientifically validated data. He eschews "hard data" from the social sciences in

favor of "terms that readers can check against their own experiences and observation."

The author states early that he wants to raise questions
rather than answer them. For me, he raises a question about
his forensics when he tries to rationalize his position about
stupidity$_1$ (as a category) by arguments which use stupidity$_2$
(in a specific instance) and stupidity$_3$ (as a position on a
vertical scale of ascending mental prowess whereon everyone
below you on the scale is relatively stupid) as if they were
identical with stupidity$_1$.

BERNARD CHALIP

Alameda, California

Preconceptions and Misconceptions

VISITORS TO THE UNITED STATES AND HOW THEY SEE US,
    by Bryant M. Wedge. Princeton, N.J.: D. Van Nostrand,
    1965. 168 pp. $4.95.

SINCE 1947, the State Department has brought between
700 and 1,900 leaders from other countries to the United
States each year as part of its Foreign Leader Program. Although many of these leaders were setting foot on U.S. soil
for the first time, they were not "seeing" America for the
first time. They had already seen the United States in movies,
books, newspapers, articles, propaganda broadcasts, etc. The
conflict between the reality of the United States and the preconceptions of these foreign leaders is the subject of this book,
which should be of special interest to all semanticists.

To explore some of the problems which confront the
American host-diplomat in communicating with these visitors,
Bryant M. Wedge and his assistants interviewed 100 escort-
interpreters, employees of the State Department who are
usually assigned to accompany each visitor during the 30- to
90-day period he is in the United States. These interviews were
supplemented by interviews with officials who also have contact with the visitors.

The misconceptions that the visitors bring with them to the United States are sometimes overwhelming. A number of African visitors, for example, were under the impression that there was systematic segregation in the United States similar to the "apartheid" program in South Africa, or that they would be lynched if they looked at a white woman. The members of one group of visitors pulled the shades in their railroad car when the train was passing through Chicago for fear they would be shot by the Al Capone gang. Others expected to see cowboys and Indians fighting in the streets.

Although these were extreme reactions, the escort-interpreters found a constant semantic problem: Words that connote one thing to Americans often connote something entirely different to foreigners. For example, "colored" is an acceptable synonym for "Negro" in the United States, but in Africa the word means mulatto, neither black nor white, and an African hesitates to identify with such a word. In French-speaking Africa, a native is politely called "un noir" ("black"), while the derogatory expression is "un negre." In Madagascar "Negro" is similar to the term "nigger," and in Nigeria "Negro" connotes "pygmy."

To help the American host over some of the more common semantic hurdles, Dr. Wedge, who is director of the Institute for the Study of National Behavior, has compiled a list of the twelve most positive and the twelve most negative words—or phrases—as perceived by the foreign visitors. The positive words, in rank order from the most positive, are: peace, progress, national sovereignty, independence, freedom, self-determination, human rights, planning, individual dignity, equality of opportunity, developing country, and government for the people. The negative words, in rank order from the most negative, are: imperialism, colonialism, intervention, exploitation, aggression, dictatorship, nuclear testing, Cold War, Chiang Kai-shek, communism, capitalism, and Mao Tse-tung.

Dr. Wedge's study found that many of the visitors were first surprised—even shocked—that their preconceptions were wrong, but thereafter they were willing to absorb the new, real picture of America. On the other hand, he found that no amount of exposure "will penetrate a closed mind, much less a hostile one. Among several thousand visitors, not a single instance was uncovered where a basically unfriendly or rigid conceptual system was said to undergo any fundamental alteration due to actual experiences during a visit."

One of the greatest barriers to understanding, the study shows, is the average visitor's lack of knowledge of the "federal" structure of the United States. Since most of the visitors come from countries with strong centralized governments, they are unable to comprehend the limitations of the U.S. central government in dealing with such problems as racial integration. They therefore conclude that our government isn't seriously committed to solving such problems.

Among Dr. Wedge's hints to Americans who find themselves in the role of host to foreign visitors are these two: (1) Abjure abstract terms and use language that makes sense to the visitor and harmonizes with his interests and experience, and (2) use demonstrations instead of verbalized information —that is, let the visitor see with his own eyes how the average American lives.

The host must first understand the semantic and political background of the visitor if he is to communicate with his guest successfully. Dr. Wedge contributes to this knowledge by discussing fully the semantic barriers to understanding that exist among Africans, Russians, Japanese, and Latin Americans.

A minor criticism of the book is that it is sometimes repetitious. Dr. Wedge, on occasion, amplifies the same point two or three times in different sections of his book.

This is a useful book. But it can perform a greater service than merely being made required reading for American hosts. It should also be made available to the visitors themselves prior to their arrival here to help them understand the semantic handicaps that both they and their American hosts bring into the experience of their American visit.

RALPH L. LOWENSTEIN

Freedom of Information Center
University of Missouri

*In Order to Make the Best**

YOU ARE NOT THE TARGET, by Laura Archera Huxley. New York: Farrar, Straus & Giroux, 1963. Copyright © 1963 by Laura Huxley. 289 pp. $4.95.

HUMAN BEINGS are multiple amphibians, living simultaneously in half a dozen radically dissimilar universes—the molecular and the ethical, the physiological and the symbolic, the world of incommunicably subjective experience and the public worlds of language and culture, of social organization and the sciences. Because they can talk and think and pass on accumulated knowledge from one generation to the next, human beings are incomparably cleverer than the cleverest of animals. But because they often talk foolishly, think illogically and reverence pseudo-knowledge as though it were revealed truth, they can also be incomparably more stupid, more unhappy, more cruel and rapacious than the most mindlessly savage of dumb beasts. Brutes are merely brutal; men and women are capable of being devils and lunatics. They are no less capable of being fully human—even, occasionally, of being a bit more than fully human, of being saints, heroes and geniuses.

Deliberate and consistent malevolence is rare. Most of us mean well and would prefer, on the whole, to behave decently. But alas, good intentions ineptly carried out are the very things with which, proverbially, hell is paved. We can talk, we know the big words; nothing, therefore, is easier for us than to enunciate a lofty ideal. The difficulties arise when we try to translate the ideal into practice. To achieve our noble ends, what are the means which must be employed? Precisely how do we intend to implement our high purposes? What must multiple amphibians do in order to make the best, for themselves and for other multiple amphibians, of all their strangely assorted worlds?

These are the questions to which, for the last two or three

---

* Copyright © 1963 by Laura Huxley. This review, originally published as a foreword to Mrs. Huxley's book, is reprinted by her permission and that of the publishers, Farrar, Straus & Giroux, Inc.

years, I have been trying to find answers plausible enough to take their place in a kind of Utopian and yet realistic phantasy about a society (alas hypothetical) whose collective purpose is to help its members to actualize as many as possible of their desirable potentialities [now published under the title, *Island*. Harper and Row, 1962]. The writing of such a book requires a good deal of preliminary research—or, if that is too solemn a word, let us say a good deal of miscellaneous reading and the picking of a considerable variety of brains. Greek history, Polynesian anthropology, translations from Sanskrit and Chinese of Buddhist texts, scientific papers on pharmacology, neuro-physiology, psychology and education, together with novels, poems, critical essays, travel books, political commentaries and conversations with all kinds of people, from philosophers to actresses, from patients in mental hospitals to tycoons in Rolls-Royces—everything went into the hopper and became grist for my Utopian mill. In a word, *je prends mon bien ou je le trouve,* I take my property where I find it—and sometimes it happens that I find it very close at hand. For example, I discovered that some of the clearest and most practical answers to certain of my questions were being given by my wife in the "Recipes for Living and Loving," which she was composing for the benefit of those who came to her for psychological aid and counsel. Some of her recipes (for example, those for the Transformation of Energy) have found their way, almost unmodified, into my phantasy. Others have been changed and developed to suit the needs of my imaginary society and to fit into its peculiar culture. This literary debt is one which, along with all my other non-literary debts to the author of *You Are Not the Target,* I am happy to acknowledge.

ONE FINAL WORD. Though my debt is literary, the material I have borrowed is more and other than mere literature. These recipes work. I have tried some of them on myself and have found them remarkably effective. And no wonder. Doing these recipes, I was forced to practice what, as a theorist of human nature, I had always preached—the great truth (so obvious once it has been recognized, but so constantly ignored even by those who ought to know better) that the life-problems of a multiple amphibian are many-faceted and, if they are to be solved, must be attacked simultaneously from many different angles.

The man of letters is tempted to live too exclusively in only a few of the universes to which, as a multiple amphibian, he has access. The schizophrenic is one who has completely succumbed to this temptation and who exists in a strange shadow world, a kind of homemade limbo. While lecturing at the Menninger Foundation in the spring of 1960, I was able, on a number of occasions, to meet with a group of far-out schizophrenics, who were receiving, every few days, an hour of music therapy. On several of these occasions I managed to induce all the members of this group to practice a version, somewhat modified to suit the peculiar circumstances, of the recipe "Your Favorite Flower." The results were dramatic. With only one exception, these inhabitants of the shadowy other-world of mental illness returned, temporarily at least, to the substantial, human reality of here-and-now. A few minutes before, there had been no communication; now we could talk together. Questions were asked and answered.

Personal anecdotes were recounted. Comments (often thoroughly sensible and to the point) were volunteered. The fact that men and women so extremely sick could respond in this way, albeit only for an hour or two, to one of these recipes was a remarkable tribute to the essential validity of what may be called the recipe-oriented approach. If far-out schizophrenics can get so much, how much more can the rest of us expect to receive? What can the recipe-oriented approach do for the mildly neurotic, the people with manageable problems, the healthy ones who would like to be still healthier and aspire to actualize yet more of their potentialities for love and intelligence and creativeness? There is only one way of finding out. "If *you* work, they work."

ALDOUS HUXLEY

What's in a Name?

THE THREE CHRISTS OF YPSILANTI, by Milton Rokeach. New York: Knopf, 1964. 332 pp. $5.95.

MUCH has been written in recent years about individual "identity," from religious, psychological, and existential points of view: what kind of person is one, what is significant and unique about a given individual, where does he stand in relation to others.

In Milton Rokeach's recent book, *The Three Christs of Ypsilanti,* identity in its simpler sense—but with its more complex ramifications—is explored, manipulated experimentally for scientific purposes, and further explored.

In Michigan's state mental hospital are three men, a farmer, a clerk, and an electrician, each of whom claims to be Jesus Christ. What will happen when these men come face to face, knowing that, by force of a primitive logic clear even to the psychotic, three individuals cannot possess the same identity?

Earlier, the psychologist Robert Lindner had reported that when two mentally ill "Marys" had confronted each other, one had relinquished her psychotic identity in deference to the other, and had thereupon recovered her rightful identity, and thereby her sanity.

Whether or not the outcome would be so fortunate in this instance was of secondary interest to Dr. Rokeach, who is a social psychologist. His main purpose was a scientific investigation of the nature of belief systems, how these change, and how the changes might affect behavior.

The author reports the intriguing fact that among children the game of "let's pretend" (that he or the parent is someone else) is pleasing only so long as the child can be assured that it is only a game. The author offers convincing evidence in some anecdotes from his experience with a number of children, including his own, that if the game is persisted in by an adult for more than a few moments, the child's primitive belief system is threatened; he becomes annoyed, then panicky; and he begs that all concerned resume their correct identities.

For purposes of Dr. Rokeach's project, the three "Christs" were assigned to the same sitting room on the ward, adjacent beds and places at the table, and work tasks which would bring them into close proximity on a daily basis. In addition, a more intensive interaction was provided for by means of a daily "discussion group" in which the men met with the author and one or two assistants for about an hour daily. These meetings could not be made compulsory, of course, but the men adapted to this new part of their routine fairly easily. Occasionally, one of them would be absent, or escape to the toilet for a good part of the hour, but for the most part they attended regularly and participated increasingly. This group met some of the patients' needs also: for human companionship and contact and for a relief from the relentless monotony and boredom of institutional life. The things the men talked of during these meetings sketch the individual character of each man and comprise a good deal of the material of the book.

A S THE STUDY progressed, a second purpose emerged: to investigate the ways in which belief systems and behavior might be changed through sending the patient-subjects messages purporting to come from positively regarded persons who were part of their delusional systems. These included, among others, an uncle and a Tibetan wife.

The 19th century physician, Bleuler, who wrote the first classic work on schizophrenia, claimed that such patients use a "double-entry bookkeeping" system for their delusions; that is, at some level they know what is reality and what is fantasy. Though initially the author and his co-workers were inclined to view this as quite possible, their experiments in contriving letters, phone calls, messages, and meetings finally led them to reject this hypothesis.

On many occasions the author had asked the men "Who else believes what you believe?" or some variation of this question. Their answer definitely indicated that they knew no one else believed their assertions. However, this in no way negated or weakened their beliefs. One man, for example, said: "Truth is truth, no matter if only one person speaks it."

The author states further that as a result of his own experience with the drug LSD, which enabled him to experience some hallucinations of his own, he feels convinced that there is no pretense, no "double entry" involved. He asserts that even though he knew he was under the influence of a powerful drug and that the reality of his experience would not be supported by social consensus, nevertheless, nothing which anyone said or did could convince him that the experience was not actually happening to him.

Are there applications or generalizations of the knowledge gained from the study of the three Christs to normal people?

Current theories in psychiatry are coming more frequently to consider the many forms of mental illness as different manifestations of a disturbance of the sense of identity. The eminent psychoanalyst, Erik Erikson, extended the psychoanalytic theory of personality development by describing the unfolding of the self as a series of identity achievements and crises in the life of the individual, from infancy through adulthood.

One does not have to adopt an overtly psychotic identity to manifest such a disturbance. From the anomie that existential psychologists describe, through amnesia, fugue states, and multiple personality, to severe schizophrenia with its dissolution of ego boundaries and loss of ego feeling—all involve identity. The present study is unique, emphasizes the author, only in that it deals with extremes of loneliness, alienation, and social anomie. In addition, it is unique in being the only written account of the confrontation of three persons with the same delusional identity.

What's in a name. . .?

By renouncing their real names these men sought to obliterate their existing identities, and by appropriating a new name —that of Jesus Christ—they sought to acquire a new identity. As a defense against deep feelings of inferiority and worthlessness, what better identity to assume than that of a man revered and divine, yet misunderstood and martyred?

"In giving up their ego identifies," comments the author, "Clyde, Joseph, and Leon gave up the rose as well as the name; they gave up their group identities, their identifications with family, religion, country, and occupation. . . ." They abandoned these in favor of a more grandiose identity and more interesting, significant, and satisfactory families, beliefs, nationalities, and occupations.

WHAT WERE the end results of the confrontation? Did the three Christs show any indication of giving up their delusions? The confrontations were upsetting and threatening to the men, and all three responded to them—especially Leon, the youngest of the three, whose belief system underwent some revision and showed some refinement and restructuring. However, the three Christs did not recover their sanity as a result of the identity confrontations, thus not substantiating the contention that it is impossible for two or more objects to occupy the same psychological space at the same time.

Although the men responded and changed somewhat as a result of the experimental interventions (and perhaps the large amount of attention and interest shown them), as the author says, "We, unlike the atomic physicists, have not as yet learned how to control reactions in order to achieve an enduring socially desirable end."

These "Christs" became psychotic with good reason and stayed that way for probably equally good ones. For the road back is a long and arduous one and must be motivated by something substantial and compelling. At the time that Leon came nearest to facing a choice about which way to go, the author describes his dilemma with a touching poem by a schizophrenic patient:

> There! There is no cave.
> It is gone.
> But where did I go?
> I cannot find me.
> Where am I?
> Lost.
>
> Yes, I want the cave,
> There, I know where I am.
> I can grope, in the dark,
>   and feel the cave walls.
> And the people, there, know I'm there,
>   and they step on me, by mistake,—
> I think, I hope.
> But, outside—
> Where am I?

For the casual reader the book may not be awfully fascinating and absorbing, as much of it contains a patient chronicling of daily events and gradual changes, as well as verbatim transcriptions of conversations with and between the patients. The author's discussion of his project in relation to theoretical considerations, such as identity and primitive belief systems, and his tying it to other relevant, known events, at the beginning and end of the book, are perhaps the most absorbing.

The interested reader will find the author's treatment of identity worthwhile, I think, from the point of view of names, labels, beliefs, self-concepts, and consequent behavior.

NANCY MEHL PETERSON

Sausalito, California

People Who Knew Who They Were

ISLAND, by Aldous Huxley. New York: Harper and Brothers, 1962. 335 pp. $5.

A LDOUS HUXLEY'S *Island,* set in the Pacific in the current cold war period, featured a people who sustained a low rate of neurosis and cardiovascular trouble and behaved as though they were essentially sane and naturally good.

The Palinese lived according to a code expounded by the Old Raja of Pala in "Notes on What's What, and on What It might Be Reasonable To Do about What's What." In his notes the Raja had written: "Good being is in the knowledge of who in fact one is in relation to all experiences. So be aware —aware in every context, at all times and whatever, creditable or discreditable, pleasant or unpleasant, you might be doing or suffering. This is the only yoga, the only spiritual exercise worth practicing."

Readers of Huxley's *Island* who are familiar with principles of general semantics and aspects of Zen, Mahayana, and Tantra should find mythical Pala well within their ken as a land where even the Mynahs avowed the key to the good life with their calls: "Attention! Attention!" "Here and now, boys: here and now!"

The Mynahs had long ago been taught to repeat these expressions by the old Raja and his English doctor, Andrew Mac-Phail, to help keep the Palinese paying attention to what's happening now. Through succeeding generations (over 100 years) of Rajas and MacPhails, the Palinese developed a way of life blending the best of Western and Oriental cultures.

Huxley describes Pala through the character William Asquith Farnaby, who worked for the newspapers of Lord Aldehyde in England. Aldehyde was also chief of Southeast Asia Petroleum, and he commissioned Farnaby, with the promise of a bonus of two thousand pounds, to sound out Palinese authorities on the prospects of obtaining oil rights in Pala.

Through an accident, Farnaby got to Pala and into the protective arms of the very people he had contracted to subvert.

The MacPhails and assorted Palinese introduced Farnaby to the intricacies of the island's political, economic, and social structure. Not conversant with general semantics or aspects of Buddhism, as were Mr. Huxley and as are readers of *ETC.,* Farnaby, despite his handicap, became entranced and almost converted to belief by what he saw in Pala.

One of his co-conspirators, Abdul Pierre Bahu, Ambassador of Rendang and agent of Rendang's oil-minded dictator, Colonel Dipa, assessed Palinese policies as being "perfectly wrong because all too perfectly right. . . . perfectly right, because so perfectly designed to make every man, woman, and child on this enchanting island as perfectly free and happy as it's possible to be." However, because Palinese policies were "out of context," he explained, "they've become completely irrelevant to the present situation in the world in general and Pala in particular."

Together Farnaby and Bahu worked with Rani, a former princess of Rendang and the Queen mother of Pala, and Murugan, the 18-year-old Raja of Pala, to put Pala back into context with the world and, of course, into harmony with Southeast Asia Petroleum. But Farnaby proceeded with increasing reluctance and regrets. Between the start of his mission and its successful culmination, he had admiring looks into the world of "science and sanity" that was Pala.

Farnaby found that while there were no "best answers" in the Palinese way of life, the people under the democratic guidance of consecutive generations of Rajas and MacPhails had learned to employ hypnosis, birth control, eugenics, biology, and other sciences of life to integrate the whole mind-body of the individual.

As Tantriks the Palinese didn't renounce the world or deny its value; didn't try to escape into a Nirvana apart from life. They accepted the world, made use of it, made use of everything they did and of everything that happened to them, of all the things they saw and heard and tasted and touched as so many means to their liberation from the prison of themselves.

Palinese biochemist Ranga explained to Farnaby, "When we make statements, we follow them up with a list of operations that can be used to test the validity of what we've been saying."

Through maithuna, described as the yoga of love, population control, a food supply insured through experimental science and uses of applied physics such as electricity, social devices such as mutual adoption clubs in which children were given more room for adjustments in the process of growing up, and psychological devices such as destiny control, the people of Pala, Farnaby learned, were trying to live best in the here and now instead of living somewhere else in some homemade imaginary universe.

IN EXPLAINING Pala's program, Dr. Robert MacPhail indicated that the first MacPhail on the Island and the Raja, whose life he had saved, had worked together to make a better world. They had begun as pain relievers and then had developed agriculture and language, using English as a second language for business, science, and speculative philosophy. In the ensuing years, they, and those who had followed, had chosen to adapt Pala economy and technology to human beings.

"We import what we can't make, but we make and import only what we can afford. And what we can afford is limited not merely by our supply of pounds and marks and dollars, but also primarily—primarily," Dr. MacPhail insisted, "by our wish to be happy, our ambition to become fully human." In Pala maximum efficiency wasn't a categorical imperative. The Palinese thought first of human beings and their satisfactions. Whenever there was a choice between mechanical efficiency and human satisfaction, the Palinese chose the latter.

From Vijaya, MacPhail's laboratory assistant, and from the doctor himself, Farnaby learned about Moksha-medicine, the reality revealer, the truth and beauty pill used to do something to the silent areas of the brain and which "opens some kind of neurological sluice and so allows a larger volume of Mind with a large 'M' to flow into your mind with a small 'm.' "

Palinese education aimed at developing boys and girls, not for mass consumption nor for strengthening the state, but for actualization, for being turned into full blown human beings. The individual was educated as a whole mind-body along with the symbol-using intellect. Palinese superiority did not lie in symbolic expression but in the art of adequately experiencing, the art of becoming more intimately acquainted with all the worlds that as human beings they found themselves inhabiting.

The Palinese knew that man couldn't help making symbols. They knew that was what the human brain was for—"to turn the chaos of given experience into a set of manageable symbols." They believed that when sometimes the symbols corresponded fairly closely to some aspects of the external reality behind their experience, then they had science and common sense. When on the contrary the symbols had almost no connection with external reality, the result was paranoia and delirium. A talent for manipulating symbols, they found, tempted its possessor into habitual symbol manipulation which often could be an obstacle in the way of concrete experiencing and the reception of gratuitous graces.

Palinese education employed games and puzzles to teach children, among other things, that scientific thinking should be in terms of probability, that old eternal verities should be viewed as high degree of likeness, and that immutable laws of nature should be seen as statistical averages.

As Farnaby was learning more delightful facts about the

use in Palinese education of ecology, applied general semantics, devices for letting off dangerous heads of steam raised by anger and frustration, the foreign forces of industrial production and the oil that greases the wheels moved inexorably on in the takeover of Pala.

While Farnaby participated in a long talk-session and Moksha-medicine with Dr. MacPhail's daughter-in-law; Murugan, now come of age as Raja, Rani, queen mother and would-be leader of a world spiritual crusade, and Colonel Dipa took over Pala. Even though Farnaby will get his oil money bonus, the reader may wonder whether when the newsman goes back to his Western World home he will continue to be fully aware of "what he thinks he is, and whether it will help him to become aware of what he is in fact." As the story ended thus, and as the author is now gone, we cannot expect the *Island Revisited*. But the *Island* will remain as a hopeful contrast to the *Brave New World*.

ARTHUR F. NICHOLSON
Shippensburg, Pennsylvania

Understanding vs. Imagination

LITERATURE, PHILOSOPHY, AND THE IMAGINATION, by Albert William Levi. Bloomington: Indiana University Press, 1962. 346 pp. $7.95.

IN *Literature, Philosophy, and the Imagination,* Levi presents a most erudite justification of the humanities. He is concerned with the dualism that has plagued philosophy since the beginning of the conflict between the natural sciences and the humanities; more especially, he is concerned with the conflicting views of man that the two disciplines suggest. His starting point is the philosophy of Kant and Kant's treatment of the scientific understanding in his *Critique of Pure Reason* and of the humanistic imagination in his *Critique of Judgment*. Levi's point is that "understanding" and "imagination" are two separate functions of the cognitive needs of man, and that "essentially the purposes of the two enterprises are different, and they are grounded respectively in the nuclear operations of the understanding and the imagination." He finds understanding (or science) and imagination (or the humanities) basically irreconcilable. The "chain of understanding" is concerned with matters of fact and a reliance on the principle of causation, whereas the "humanistic complex" is anthropomorphic and is concerned with teleology and drama.

Levi carefully documents his disagreement with the positivists' view of man and his relation to the world of natural phenomena. (In fact, his documentation is so thorough that it presents an excellent summary of modern philosophical thought.) He sees this view as one which is primarily "valueless" when compared with the "propensity toward teleological interpretation" which man inherently has and which is reflected in the humanities. It is the imagination which is concerned with "purposiveness" and "drama" in life.

Drawing from Santayana and Gilbert Ryle, Levi suggests that to meet his cognitive needs, man needs two maps of reality. However, despite the similarities which may seem to exist between the two "maps," they are composed of different vocabularies which are addressed to entirely different problems. Levi gives an interesting scheme of the confrontation of the two language maps:

THE SCIENTIFIC CHAIN OF MEANING (The Language of the Understanding)	THE HUMANISTIC COMPLEX (The Language of the Imagination)
"True" and "false" propositions.	"Reality" and "appearance."
The problem of "error."	The problem of "illusion."
"Causality" and "scientific law."	"Destiny" and "human purpose."
"Prediction" and "chance."	"Fate" and "fortune."
"Fact"—"matter of fact."	"Drama" and "the dramatic event."
"Competition"—"biological growth."	"Tragedy."
The "stasis" or "equilibrium" of systems.	"Peace."

For example, the scientist is concerned with the truth and falsity of propositions, the poet with the appearances and realities of the world, and so the problem that one deals with under the rubric of "error," the other must consider under the heading of "illusion."

For Levi, an empirical approach to all the problems of the "human condition" is an unsatisfactory one: It largely ignores man's tremendous drive to find purpose and drama in his existence. He says that the imagination develops a metaphysics, though not a mysticism, which makes life bearable. It is through the imagination that man expresses his sense of purposiveness and drama in life, and the attempts of many philosophers to find the same attributes in a scientific or empirical system are unconvincing. This thesis is developed throughout the book by the analyses of a very large number of important works of literature.

The student of general semantics will find much that he may argue with in Levi's presentation. At the same time, he will find much that is provocative. The dualism that Levi presents is one that is still pertinent.

ALTON A. HOBGOOD

San Francisco State College

Organic Teaching

TEACHER, by Sylvia Ashton-Warner. New York: Simon and Schuster, 1963. 224 pp. $5.

TWO STRUGGLES are combined in this one lively and spontaneous outpouring by Sylvia Ashton-Warner, and the telling of each struggle enhances the difficulties and importance of the other.

One struggle is that of the fierce, brown Maori children of New Zealand to cross the verbal bridge from one culture to another. It is not just learning to read. "It's the bridge," says the author, "from the known to the unknown; from a native culture to a new; and, universally speaking, from the inner man out."

Sylvia Ashton-Warner finds that she cannot tell a child what a word means when he uses it, but she *can* listen to him when he uses it. To help her Maoris and Pakehas* she takes key vocabularies from the children themselves. Her children *love and fear*. Made free to caption their own inner visions, they present their teacher with their organic reading and organic writing vocabularies. "Kiss," "frightened," "ghost," "Mummy," "Daddy," proved to be words in each of their key vocabularies. Special words serve needs according to the children's experiences—"the fear words dominating the design, a few sex words, the person interest, and the temper of the century . . . bomb, kiss, brothers, butcher knife, gaol, love, dance, cry, fight, hat, bulldog, touch, wild piggy."

It takes tremendous energy for a Maori child to achieve a love of reading *and* comfort in the new culture. It takes energy to avoid the development of aversion to the written word, and the neurotic "retreat to the mat" of some educated Maoris. "Teacher" accomplishes this by using the energy and experience direct from the children. As the author says:

First words must have intense meaning for a child.

Pleasant words won't do. Respectable words won't do. They must be words organically tied up, organically born from the dynamic life itself.

First books must be made of the stuff of the child himself, whatever and wherever the child.

How would New Zealand children get on if all their reading material were built from the life of African blacks?

The author found that words well chosen turned out to be "one-look words" and "one-word sentences," or even "one-word books."

Teacher's children choose their own key vocabularies and write and read their own first books. But one more step is needed to insure a stable introduction to "Janet and John." Miss Ashton-Warner experimented for six years to produce the culture-security of her Maori Transitional Readers, draw-

---

* White persons.

ing the stories, illustrations, and attitudes of the readers from the children she taught.

"We play, eh? Me and you, eh?" say the Maoris. "Let us play," say "Janet and John." The author's children accomplished the mechanics of reading first in a familiar verbal and pictorial setting, ". . . and from this experience he can carry within him a confidence to any other reading book; with or without the third dimension, with or without the pa [village] temperament and with or without turquoise rain." From the experience to "Janet and John" can be a step of delight. For many of these children the struggle is won and the bridge is crossed.

THERE IS another struggle pictured in this restless book about education. This is Sylvia Ashton-Warner's long effort, not only to develop her organic teaching methods, but to bring about their use in New Zealand schools. Assumptions, generalizations, pre-judgments, and resistance to change are her opponents. "We think in sentences," she is reminded, when trying to make it clear that different sorts of people think in different sorts of sentences. "The Maoris are very erratic," prophesy local New Zealanders. Deep prejudice is felt. "It makes us very shy and sensitive," says a Maori friend.

"Organic reading" may be a new *description* for an educational method, but the *method* of *Teacher* is not new, and Miss Ashton-Warner is the first to admit it. However, the reader will find here a fresh, new experiencing of an old effort to communicate with children about communicating. To a teacher, *Teacher* can give ideas, methods, and a fresh slant. To any reader, it can give insights into teaching in New Zealand, Maoris and Maori children, and children anywhere.

NANCY SAVIDGE

San Francisco

Francis P. Chisholm—Teacher of Teachers

SIRS: On March 23, 1965 the International Society for General Semantics lost a distinguished and dedicated member in the death of Francis P. Chisholm. The loss was greater for the Wisconsin State University at River Falls and for those students today and tomorrow who will never come under his influence.

Francis P. Chisholm was a teacher of teachers. I know of no student who didn't leave his class with the feeling that he had experienced the presence of a great and different kind of man. I say "different" because there were some who could not understand the man or his lectures, who could not understand why "truth" was not presented for them to record in their notebooks for use that semester, who could not understand why their petty concerns and questions were so seriously considered and explored. Those who could not understand thought he was a kind fool. But all the while they missed what he was really like. They were not being treated as "students" but as unique, somehow-important students with a question. And I'll bet these same students who didn't understand, are teachers today who are teaching "students,"—who are teaching "4th graders" and not this particular individual 4th grader.

Francis P. Chisholm was a teacher of teachers. Those who were able to understand—and I think that portion was predominant—experienced being treated as individuals, as equally important for what insights they might contribute in any class discussion. I am sure there were many of us who lost some false security when we discovered that our "forever and eternally true" ideas of what the world was like weren't really so useful or so true. We presented our arguments and he listened. And he made us learn to listen, as well. In the course of a semester, we didn't expect "truth" and he didn't have to defend not giving it to us. We began to have a mutual concern—the search for new insights, the search for knowledge. Francis P. Chisholm, the man, gave us tools for this search. He taught us humility and patience and tolerance because he possessed these qualities and, I think, somehow expected that sooner or later we would too. Maybe of more value than any of these, he taught us to laugh. A strange thing, you might say, to teach teachers. He loved to be caught in his own foibles as much as he enjoyed pointing to those of his fellow men. He joked about things we couldn't do anything about— like the weather—and somehow pretended we could. He wrote his "famous" laws (e.g. Chisholm's Second Law of Human Interaction—Any time things appear to be going better, you have overlooked something.) with a kind of delight that man was what he was, and that was quite good enough. The fame he could have had, he never sought. But he couldn't have had fame, even if he had wanted to—he was too busy being a teacher of teachers.

RICHARD H. NAVARRE

Mount Senario College
Ladysmith, Wisconsin

Transmission of Information

SIRS: Tickled by Bill Haney's results with the serial transmission of information (*ETC.*, March 1964), I recently set up a similar experiment in my report writing class.

Instead of Haney's "cat" cartoon, however, I restructured the series, feeling that my students would be more readily convinced if the message were verbal. From reports that the trainees had submitted as representative of their work, I selected this sentence: "Nearly all the work is done in the engine room by a combination of shop men and engine crew—seldom find good mechanic and bookkeeper."

The sentence seemed to contain the same lack of clarity, the same distortion of details evident in Haney's line drawing.

If Haney's results of the stimulus picture were accurate, we could expect to see his principles verified: details would be left out; others would be added; still others would be altered. All in the name of "better" communication.

And we'd be right.

The students, all college graduates, all selected for their communications skills, were told only that they were taking part in "a little test." Four of them were selected and sent out of the room. The first man saw the test sentence for thirty seconds, long enough to read it several times. Then he was told to transmit the information in a report to the next man. Here's how the report "improved."

1. Men in the engine room consist of maintenance men and some mechanics but would make very poor secretaries.

2. Men in the maintenance room consist (of) well trained mechanists and mechanics but they would make very poor secretaries.

3. Men in the Maintenance Department make excellent machinists and mechanics but make very bad secretaries.

4. Men in the maintenance department make excellent machinists and mechanics but have lousy secretaries.

After seeing the results of the experiment, the men seemed to take a surprisingly vigorous interest in the material of the class.

ROBERT B. MOUNTS

Caterpillar Tractor Co.
Peoria, Illinois

Language and Attitudes

SIRS: Sometimes one has highly personal insights into semantic problems which seem to have some universality. I have recently been in a situation which, as a long-time reader of *ETC.*, I think may interest you.

Not long ago, after much thought, soul-searching, and cold-blooded calculation, I left my position as safety supervisor with a major railroad. I am 54 years old and so gave up my rights to the company retirement plan, though I may qualify for a portion of the Railroad Retirement Act pension at age 60. However, I am not so adventurous as I may seem since I have some savings and was recently the beneficiary of a small legacy. My wife is sympathetic to my decision, and we have no dependents.

The semantic problems are concerned principally with the language and attitudes involved in telling employers, friends, and relations of my decision, and with their responses.

I have myself used the word "quitting" to describe my action, in preference to "retiring," because the word "retire" seems to connote leaving the world of affairs, putting up one's feet, and relaxing. On the other hand, "quit" is not the *mot juste;* it seems a bit un-American—running away, leaving the fight to others. It has a wilful sound—impulsive, hasty. And "seeking other employment" won't work, because that means getting a job with another company.

What I am doing is painting and writing.

To most business associates this is a highly questionable enterprise. Painters and writers are odd-balls; painters especially are always peculiar and generally immoral; both are lazy, unstable, bearded types.

IN REVIEWING the comments made by friends and business associates, I find that the particular word I used to designate my move hasn't mattered as much as I anticipated: each person has put his own interpretation on my action in accordance with his own predilections; each has decided what I am *in fact* going to do and why I left, quit, or retired.

In the opinion of one or two I have successfully hidden my playboy nature for twenty years—I'm a gay dog bustin' loose. To others I'm fundamentally lazy, a trait I concealed only partially through the years. Still others, including some business associates, apparently take the move at its face value —that is, the value I put on it.

With all who were interested I was fairly candid: I explained that this was no idle whim, that I was prepared for it, that my wife understood, that I would be busy, that painting and writing take time and thought and effort. Some were most concerned about finances; to these I explained that I expect to augment our income with earnings from my work.

Others were strong on the psychological aspects of the plan. These had been reading some of the popular articles on the psychological problems of the "retired person." It's difficult to adjust to the irregular hours, self-indulgence, and boredom of retirement. Was I prepared to occupy my time and not get introspective and moony? Had I heard about old so-and-so who retired in March, was in the hospital by the first of May, and died in June?

THE least satisfactory were the I-guess-you-know-what-you're-doing ones. The financial ones I could reassure; the psychological ones I could convince that, since my college years were spent in studying art, and since most of my professional life had been devoted to putting thoughts into words, I was not unprepared to keep out of mischief. But to have someone say, just a little gloomily, "Well, I guess you know what you're doing" is to leave little to say in response but "Yes, I guess I do." And who knows what he is doing?

All in all it has been a most interesting and rewarding experience. There were many surprises: "stodgy" souls who understood and joined in with the idea immediately, casual acquaintances who seemed to know before I spoke what I wanted and why, "business types" who were admiring and envious. But most satisfactory of all were the friends who had no hesitation in giving enthusiastic approval.

PETER OAKESHOTT

Oakland, California

A Non-Aristotelian Ethic?

SIRS: I am writing about something which has interested me for several years—a concern which has recently been restimulated by the "objectivist ethics" of Ayn Rand. I have long felt that the failure of philosophers of this century to attempt to provide a meaningful ethic was a mixed blessing. We have thus avoided the dangers of arbitrary ethic, but a vacuum, partially and variously filled, has resulted.

My feeling is that our psychologists (broadly conceived) are in an excellent position to provide an ethic, more specifically, psychologists who endorse the principles of general semantics or work within similar or closely related frameworks. There is a very clear ethic in the writings of Korzybski, Wendell Johnson, Irving Lee, Hayakawa, Carl Rogers, A. H. Maslow, and others of similar outlook.

The foregoing is prologue to the following questions. Has anyone written a statement of ethics based on non-aristotelian principles? Is there any interest in such a venture? Would there be any interest in establishing a counterpart to Rand's *Objectivist Newsletter* for the regular examination of problems of living and current events in a non-A framework? I would be most interested in reactions from *ETC.* readers.

GEORGE MELHUS

Assistant Chief, Rehabilitation Services
State of Illinois, Department of Mental Health
Chicago, Illinois

The Role of Symbols in Human Behavior

SIRS: Dr. Dettering's article, "Our Symbol-Centered Universe," (*ETC.*, March 1965) poses many problems for the study of the role of symbols in human behavior. I agree that the pervasiveness of symbols must always be kept in mind, but I think that Dr. Dettering has overstated the case. In this connection, it is interesting to note, in the same issue of *ETC.*, some of Statton Rice's quotes from Northrop's *Man, Nature, and God,* such as: "No words mean or can say anything, except as one knows, with inexpressible and unsayable immediacy, what the words are pointing at or showing, independently of the words themselves." Here we have the basis of a good debate. I would like to hear more of Dettering's view, and particularly to have him clarify his use of "symbol" and "symbolic" in the examples he gives in his article. Undoubtedly the examples are to be considered simplifications, but it appears to me that they operate so as to cast doubt upon the basic ideas expressed in the article.

I will set forth my criticisms of the examples with the hope that Dr. Dettering will clarify his analyses.

Example No. 1 (The Rosetta Stone): Dettering says that to us it is a symbolic artifact, while to a camel driver it might have been no more than a slab of curiously scratched basalt. But even we can classify it differently, not arbitrarily, but depending on our purposes. It "is" a symbolic artifact only when we are considering the engravings on it in relation to certain symbol systems. If we are studying the crystalline structure it "is" only a particular example of basalt. I do not see that this example shows that "it is easy to view symbols as plain events of nature." How can you view units of a symbol system as plain events of nature unless you change the purpose of your view, and thus the classification system you employ? You are, of course, free to make the change, but this does not clear the distinction between symbols and non-symbols. You are not viewing a *symbol* as a plain event of nature; you have changed the frame of reference, and the question as to whether what we are dealing with is often used as a unit of a symbol system is irrelevant.

Example No. 2 (The use of the sun in the rebus-like sentence, "Astronomers say the * * * has spots right now."): In the symbol system of the English language, the actual sun is the referent of the word "sun." If we suggest the word by pointing to the referent, does this mean that we now must regard the actual sun as the symbol and the word "sun" as the referent? I do not think so. It is only by virtue of common knowledge of the symbol system of the English language that this suggestion can transmit the idea, and in that frame of reference it is the word that is the symbol.

Example No. 3 (The substitution of a dime for the missing bishop in a set of chessmen.): The players have agreed to the substitution, so in their private modification of the symbol system usually used by chess players, the dime is *a symbol* for the white queen's bishop. To say, in an exposition of this nature, that "the dime has indeed *become* the white queen's bishop," or that "an object . . . *is* the bishop when it *functions* as the bishop," is to make use of the verb "to be" in a way that confuses the issue. Why must we agree that an object "becomes a particular symbol" when it becomes a symbol for the symbol? It should furthermore be noted that it is only *within a symbol system* that the object has "become" a symbol at all. As a unit of a symbol system (an abstraction) and inseparable from the system, the object can be said to "be" a symbol, but to imply that this has a bearing on the "boundary line" between the world of symbols and the world of non-symbols is to confuse levels of abstraction.

THE simple approach "X is a symbol because I am going to let it stand for Y" is clear enough at the usual level of discourse, but in an article discussing "reality," or when we discuss whether X is an ink mark or a symbol, we must make further distinctions and qualifications.

Perhaps Professor Dettering will give us some examples that more exactly set forth his ideas of the nature of symbols and of the symbolic process. We need to know such things if we (or Professor Northrop) are to agree that "It is practically tautologous to say that our cognitive knowledge and certainty about the world, even about our immediate sensations, rests on our exercise of sybmols. . . ."

CECIL R. WELTE

Oaxaca, Mexico

Undergraduate Education at a Large State University

SIRS: While a graduate student and part-time instructor at a typical large state university, I was impressed by the fact that undergraduates were encouraged to commit a basic semantical error. Students were conditioned to think of an education as a compact body of information which could be absorbed in four years. If, after four years, a person *is* educated, he has no reason to continue his studies. The necessary wisdom has been imparted fully.

The wholesale use of graduate students as freshman and sophomore instructors is an important cause of this erroneous attitude toward education. Since they have limited knowledge and experience, graduate students can do little more than outline and explain the textbooks for their classes. And, since they have difficulty in organizing lectures and in judging their students' abilities to grasp abstract concepts, their attempts to introduce novel ideas usually end disastrously.

Graduate students are keenly aware of their teaching inadequacies, and their insecurity is reflected in their concern regarding the grade records of their classes. Different sections of the same course are usually given the same tests. Each instructor wishes to avoid the embarrassment of finding that his students consistently score lower grades than the students of other instructors on these "combined examinations." Consequently, a wise instructor will limit his class preparations to that body of information common to all class sections of a particular course: the course textbook.

This conditioning process of restricting the intellectual horizons of the undergraduates is reinforced by the official university policy of uniformity. All sections of the same course must use the same textbook and be given the same assignments. Even the combined examinations are control devices that ensure educational uniformity. Students are not given the opportunity to discover that different teachers and textbooks present different ideas and approaches.

There is a reinforcing feedback between students and teachers. Students lose interest in ideas which they feel they are not expected to learn. A graduate student seeking the undergraduates' approval of his teaching performance is reluctant to buck student apathy by introducing ideas and approaches which are not mentioned in the textbook. (In common with other instructors, I have actually been asked why we discussed certain topics not mentioned in the textbook and not expected to appear on the combined examinations.)

Conditioning students to think of their textbooks as the basic elements in their education is particularly unfortunate. Basic textbooks rarely stimulate thought. They present the "principles" of the subject—the detailed answers to dead issues. By the time an issue is incorporated into a textbook, the argument has been so thoroughly refined by thinkers in the field that undergraduates are given little opportunity to challenge or seek new approaches. Their intellectual armaments are no match for those of the textbook writers.

Most teachers in junior and senior courses are experienced faculty members. These teachers can introduce challenging ideas and approaches. However, after students have been trained for two college years to limit their studies to their textbooks, experienced teachers find it difficult to reorient the thinking of their students. Furthermore, experienced teachers may be interested primarily in graduate instruction and personal research. Consequently, they may dispose of the chore of teaching undergraduates by presenting the same lecture material year after year. Like the textbook, their lectures eventually become so well perfected that they do not stimulate the students to think and inquire—they merely convince. Thus, even experienced teachers may frequently encourage undergraduates to conclude that their education will be *completed* once they have mastered the small funds of information to which they will have been exposed during their four-year stays at the university.

BERNARD SARACHEK

University of Detroit

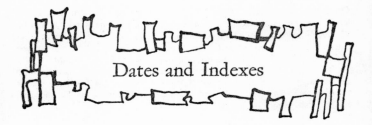

Dates and Indexes

THE NEWSLETTER BUSINESS. In the previous issue of "Dates and Indexes" it was suggested that these pages be viewed as a newsletter on general semantics. To follow up on the idea we looked up a resource on the subject, *Newsletter Writing and Publishing*, by Virginia M. Burke (Teachers College, Columbia University, 1958). Prominent in the bibliography of this reference work were the writings of Irving Lee, Wendell Johnson, and S. I. Hayakawa. A chapter on "Writing Style" includes these pertinent observations:

"*Abstraction ladders.* Living as we do in a concrete world, most of us are not happy for very long on high levels of abstraction. The healthy mind tends to learn and think by moving up and down abstraction ladders, i.e., by moving back and forth from one degree of abstraction to another. Abstraction ladders arrange related statements in order according to degrees of abstraction, beginning at the top with the most abstract and moving to the most concrete at the bottom. . . .

"One mark of effective thinkers and writers is their ability to go up and down abstraction ladders quickly and easily. When writers and speakers get stuck at the bottom levels, we may get something similar to those endless telephone chats between Mrs. Smith and Mrs. Jones—a string of unrelated specific facts leading nowhere. When speakers and writers get stuck at the top levels of the ladder, we often get abstract communication that is unappealing and difficult to follow. Aware of the up-and-down process of the normal mind, skilled speakers and writers present their material in flexible, up-and-down fashion—narrating, quoting, generalizing, illustrating, summarizing as the normal mind does. . . .

"Relationships among the levels of abstraction on which writers work are extremely important. It is not always true that the better method is to begin at high levels and move to lower levels. Nor is it sound to say that writers should always begin on low levels of abstraction and move to higher levels. But one weakness in writing which begins at high levels is the fact that it often stays at high levels when this is not necessary, without ever moving down to concrete examples or illustrations. . . ."

SEMANTICS FROM A SENATOR. Minnesota Senator Eugene J. McCarthy, in the course of an interview on the nationally televised TODAY Show (NBC-TV, May 20, 1966), made the following remark: "General Gavin's critics told him what he meant by 'enclave'— and they never gave him an opportunity to say what *he* meant."

This nicely sums up the semantic principle that the person who uses a word is the final authority on what he means by it. A hearer can only *infer* the meaning. And when this "semantic truth" is ignored, misunderstandings—failures of communication—occur. The lesson is clear: the way to find out what a particular speaker means when he uses a particular word on a particular occasion is to ask him. We are grateful to the Senator. [Lee Eisler, Coopersburg, Pa.]

WHAT'S IN A NAME? "A Viet Cong Communist trooper captured near this central coastal town [Qui Nhon] the other day was asked why he had joined the Viet Cong. He answered—freely rendered —'One day a man came to my hut in my hamlet with a list of names. My name was on the list. He said, "We need you in the Viet Cong —will you work with us?" In all my life nobody had ever used my whole name. Nobody had ever said I was needed, or asked me to do something for the people. So I joined them.' " Howard K. Smith in the San Francisco *Examiner,* August 11.

GUIDE TO PEDAGUESE, by James S. LeSure (New York: Harper and Row, 1965; 172 pp., $3.95). "Mothers of the nation's school-children, arise! And fathers, too," writes Dr. LeSure. "It's time to battle the educators with their own chief weapon—words." His "hand-book for puzzled parents" might also serve as an effective glossary for the teacher, school administrator, educational journalist, and the professional educationist, bring much of the jargon of professional education to an extensional level. Included are such topics as: *ability grouping, basal, climate for learning, creativity, disadvantaged, felt need, language arts, progressive education, self-realization, whole-child, world understandings,* etc. Not included (unfortunately): *semantics, extensionalize, abstraction ladder.* The term *abstraction* is treated this way:

"Most of us are familiar with a number of meanings for this word, especially, perhaps, in connection with modern art. I find it disconcerting, however, to encounter it as a synonym for learning as I have several times recently. Perhaps this meaning for abstraction has been around for a long time, but I don't find it in my current dictionary. I suppose the idea is that one *abstracts* significance from a process or an experience, and hence learns. What is wrong with the usual synonyms for learning that makes it necessary to dredge up another, especially one with roots as vague (abstract?) as this? But vagueness and obscurity of meaning do not deter the determined pedaguesian. They spur him on."

On "pedaguese" LeSure writes: "I first encountered 'pedaguese' when I entered a graduate school of education some years ago. One teacher among my classmates was fond of the term, but it was some years before I heard it again. Used more often by educators than by others, it is a derisive label for the jargon of the educationist, especially those among us who write textbooks and professional monographs. Unfortunately, that jargon is used all too often also by teachers and administrators in attempting to communicate with the public."

QUOTES WITHOUT COMMENT: In an interview article titled "God is Not 'Dead' " (*U.S. News and World Report*, April 25, 1966), the Rev. Billy Graham made the following statement:

"Now, my own definition of God would be that 'God is a spirit—absolute, personal, holy, infinite and eternal in His being and attributes.' And there are many, many definitions that theologians have given of God in the past. And there are some definitions in the Bible that give more than one aspect of God. But it is impossible to phrase a single, complete definition of God. No definition really satisfies me."

INTERNATIONAL NOTES. *Sprache, Denken, Wirklichkeit*, a German translation of *Language, Thought and Reality* by Benjamin Lee Whorf, has been included in *Rowohlts Deutsche Enzyklopaedie* (Munich, West Germany). . . . The second edition of *Language in Thought and Action*, by S. I. Hayakawa, has been published in England by Georgia Allen and Unwin, Ltd. . . . Sixten Flach, a director of ISGS, reports a series of lectures on "Language and Peace" given in Stockholm during the past year. Some of the topics presented: Language and Reality; Language and Society; What is General Semantics?; The Silent Language; A Report from the International Conference on General Semantics in San Francisco; Language Problems in Technical Assistance Work.

SANCTITY OF RELIGIOUS BELIEF. "The rightest terrorists have succeeded in some places. . . . A writer for *Look* notes that a community mental health services bill squeezed by in Utah, but with amendments making it a felony . . . to give psychiatric treatment to change a patient's 'concept of, belief about or faith in God.' 'What do I do,' asks a Utah psychiatrist, 'if my patient thinks he *is* God?' " *Psychiatric Quarterly.*

5000 ADULT SEX WORDS AND PHRASES, compiled and edited by John Trimble, Ph.D. (North Hollywood, Cal.: Brandon House Books, 1966. 235 pp. 95 cents.). Brandon House, a paperback publisher of such works as *Bedroom Suburb, Carnival Mistress, The Pas-*

sion Hunters, Love Me Wild, etc., has put forward "a treatise on common sexual terms in modern English idiom . . . . earthy, factual, blunt, sometimes shocking." Entries were classified according to four categories: (1) Conventional—words acceptable in polite society, i.e., *adultery, concubine, hedonism,* etc.; (2) Medical—words coined and used by members of the medical and psychological professions, i.e., *algolagnia, libido, shunamatism,* etc.; (3) Slang—terms which have not been incorporated into the English language by competent scholars and lexicographers, i.e., *call girl, swing, shack up,* etc.; (4) Vulgarisms —expressions that are strictly out of bounds in polite society, i.e., *baker flying, knock up, roll,* etc. According to the blurb on the cover "a veritable self-study course in SEX education by a professional sexologist."

DISSOLVING LANDSCAPE? Seldom have we found as provocative a course description as that presented by a prospectus of Viewpoint Institute on a lecture-workshop course, "The Creative Arts in a Dissolving Landscape," conducted by Stephen Longstreet. The course, involving a series of eight meetings, is outlined as follows:

1. *A Collage Workshop* . . . The enigma of the creative process; students participating in creating personal art-forms.

2. *Sexual Revolution and the Berkeley Rebels* . . . Puritan guilt to The Scarlet Letter; Henry Miller, Mae West, to Who's Afraid of Elizabeth Taylor; Sade and Freud revisited.

3. *How Square is Camp?* . . . The Campbell Soup Can Homosexual Revolution; from Dorian Gray's lily to the Phallus on a Hot Tin Roof; 007, Batman; LSD to Barney's Beanery as a philosophical system.

4. *The Flawed Prophets* . . . D. H. Lawrence to C. P. Snow, including Alistair Crowley, Herbert Hoover, Dali, the Lindberghs, John Cage, Dr. Strangelove, and the unfound corpse of God.

5. *Man as a Political Animal* . . . The great immortality: from the smoke filled room to Ronald Reagan; the Kennedy Legend, Mr. Johnson's War; Soupy Sales in the White House in 1968.

6. *Poe's Raven to the Naken Lunch* . . . A study of American writers: Poe-Faulknerland, the new ghetto of Mailer, Bellow, Roth, Malamud, Fiedler; old fashioned fornication from Dreiser to Hemingway.

7. *Voices in the Streets* . . . the myth of the western hero, the unroaring 20's lost generation; James Cagney meets the Warner Bros., Flight of the Okies, rise of the tabloids, death of the American newspaper, the strange birth of TIME-LIFE.

8. *Radio and Television* . . . The burial of American taste: soap opera to Peyton Place, national brainwashing, Madison Ave. style; the Huntley-Brinkley love affair; the birth of Orwell's New World.

NEVER FORGIVE, NEVER FORGET! "Editor: How fitting that
retribution should come to the Turks in the form of earthquakes
in some of the very same towns and villages where the Turks massacred
the Armenians. The old maxim, 'The sins of the fathers shall be visited
upon their sons,' is borne out to be true once again. Earl Kasabian."
From the letters column of San Francisco *Chronicle*, August 29, 1966.

EYE OF THE BEHOLDER. Herb Caen in the *Chronicle:* "In a
paternity case, it's always *his child;* in a divorce, it's always *her*
children." In a somewhat ancient clipping from the *Chronicle* (April
28, 1963) we note that two statues of British explorer David Livingstone will be demolished by the Tanganyikan government. The two
statues, standing on the north shore of Lake Nyasa and in the capital
city of Dares-Salaam, commemorate Livingstone's "discovery" of the
lake and the surrounding region. "These places had been known to
our people from the beginning of time," said the Tanganyikan spokes-
man. "Livingstone did not discover anything."

CHICAGO CHAPTER, ISGS has a "new look" this year. Board
member Eugene Colin has designed a symbol to embellish the
Chapter stationery and to be used as masthead to the newsletter, *Sign-
posts*. The September 23 meeting was devoted to a panel discussion
of the first five chapters of Eric Berne's *The Games People Play*. Following the discussion members of the study group dramatized some
of the "games" outlined in Part II of the book. Plans for 1966-1967
include a talk by Dr. Claude Coleman of Southern Illinois University,
and a seminar at Allerton Park on June 3 and 4. Dr. Thomas M.
Weiss, Arizona State University, will conduct this seminar. The 1966
seminar at Allerton Park was conducted by Earl Kelley, author of
Education for What Is Real.

Meetings of the Chicago Chapter, ISGS, are held on the fourth
Friday of each month, September through May, at the Pick-Congress
Hotel. The current board of directors includes: Alice B. Young,
Eugene Colin, Charles Stade, May Gordon, Adeline Kovitz, Dorothy
Klofkorn, Evelyn Rochetto, Carl Stoffels, and Amydelle Shah. John
Schmitt, former board member, is serving as chairman, Business Re-
search Study.

SEMANTIC THOUGHT: "Talk to a man about himself and he will
listen for hours."—Benjamin Disraeli.

VIEWPOINTS INSTITUTE, after three years on Pico Boulevard,
moved to larger quarters—at 1424 Erdis Drive, Los Angeles—to
accommodate its full schedule of daytime and evening lectures and
workshops. The Institute, a center for the study, practice and development of general semantics, presents introductory, intermediate, and
advanced courses in semantic awareness. Enrollment for all courses

during the past year was about 900, according the Ethel Longstreet, executive director.

On April 15 to 17, a week-end conference, "A Semantic Explosion —The Emperor's New Clothes Syndrome," was held at the new California Teachers Association Conference Center at Monte Corona, Lake Arrowhead. Dr. J. Samuel Bois, Stephen Longstreet, Dr. Maurice Riseling and Ethel Longstreet were workshop leaders for 100 registrants.

DETROIT SOCIETY FOR GENERAL SEMANTICS meets monthly on the third Friday of the month. Meetings are held at 8 p.m. in the Front Room (Third floor) of the G.A.R. Building, 1942 Grand River at W. Adams. Current officers: Cecilia G. Wells, president; E. E. Baggerly, vice-president; Anthony Rand, secretary; Howard Chynoweth, treasurer. For further information contact A. F. Rand, 1008 Shelby St., Detroit, 48226. Telephone 961-4814.

MONTREAL GENERAL SEMANTICS SOCIETY reports these events: a weekend seminar with J. Samuel Bois, Los Angeles, during March; the acquisition of tape recordings of lectures given by the late Wendell Johnson for use by the society; courses in general semantics being given by Gordon Allison, Roger Keast, and Paul Tremblay at the Montreal Y.M.C.A.; by David Arthurs at the Montreal Y.M.H.A.; and by Allison at the Montreal Junior Board of Trade. The October 1966 issue of *Blue Bell*—house organ of the Bell Telephone Company of Canada—features a story about the Society. Society meetings are held on the second Tuesday of each month. For information contact M.G.S.S., Post Office Box 811, Station B, Montreal, P.Q.

VERBAL LEVEL, the lively newsletter of the New York Society for General Semantics, reports on a wide range of activities and indicates that the Society is celebrating its twentieth anniversary. During September, Jesse S. Nirenberg conducted a workshop of "Getting Through to People," and Edward F. Haskell spoke on "The Relationship of General Semantics to the Unification of Science." Fall courses being given by the Society include an in-service course for teachers, "Semantics in the English Language Arts," and a team-teaching course, "Levels of Knowing and Existence," based on Harry Weinberg's book. Other general semantics courses in the area include Harry Maynard at Cooper Union, Dr. Samuel Stein at New Rochelle High School, Allen Flagg at Queens College. October activities include a session on "Creativity" and a panel discussion on "Marshall McLuhan: General Semanticists View His Ideas on Education, Culture." Offices of the New York Society: Suite 460, 230 Park Ave., New York, 10017.